Women Pleas'd by John Fletcher

A TRAGEDY-COMEDY

John Fletcher was born in December, 1579 in Rye, Sussex. He was baptised on December 20th.

As can be imagined details of much of his life and career have not survived and, accordingly, only a very brief indication of his life and works can be given.

Young Fletcher appears at the very young age of eleven to have entered Corpus Christi College at Cambridge University in 1591. There are no records that he ever took a degree but there is some small evidence that he was being prepared for a career in the church.

However what is clear is that this was soon abandoned as he joined the stream of people who would leave University and decamp to the more bohemian life of commercial theatre in London.

The upbringing of the now teenage Fletcher and his seven siblings now passed to his paternal uncle, the poet and minor official Giles Fletcher. Giles, who had the patronage of the Earl of Essex may have been a liability rather than an advantage to the young Fletcher. With Essex involved in the failed rebellion against Elizabeth Giles was also tainted.

By 1606 John Fletcher appears to have equipped himself with the talents to become a playwright. Initially this appears to have been for the Children of the Queen's Revels, then performing at the Blackfriars Theatre.

Fletcher's early career was marked by one significant failure; The Faithful Shepherdess, his adaptation of Giovanni Battista Guarini's Il Pastor Fido, which was performed by the Blackfriars Children in 1608.

By 1609, however, he had found his stride. With his collaborator John Beaumont, he wrote Philaster, which became a hit for the King's Men and began a profitable association between Fletcher and that company. Philaster appears also to have begun a trend for tragicomedy.

By the middle of the 1610s, Fletcher's plays had achieved a popularity that rivalled Shakespeare's and cemented the pre-eminence of the King's Men in Jacobean London. After his frequent early collaborator John Beaumont's early death in 1616, Fletcher continued working, both singly and in collaboration, until his own death in 1625. By that time, he had produced, or had been credited with, close to fifty plays.

Index of Contents

DRAMATIS PERSONAE
MEN
Duke of Siena, Suitor to Belvidere.
Silvio, A Gentleman of quality, servant to Belvidere.
Claudio, Silvio's friend, brother to Isabella.
Bartello, Captain of the Citadel, Uncle to Silvio.
Lopez, A sordid Usurer, the jealous Husband of Isabella.
Lords of Florence.
Lords of Siena.
Counsellors.
Courtiers.
Penurio, A hungry servant to Lopez.
Soto, A merry servant to Claudio.
A Farmer, Father to Soto.
Captain.
Soldiers of the Guard.
A Clarke.
Bomby, An enemy to Watches and May-poles.
Morris-dancers.
Masquers.
WOMEN
Dutchess of Florence.
Belvidere, A virtuous Princess, daughter to the Duchess in love with Silvio.

Rodope, wife to Bartello.
Isabella, Wife to Lopez, and Sister to Claudio.
Jaquenet, servant to Isabella.
Two Gentlewomen.

SCENE: Florence.

ACTUS PRIMUS

SCÆNA PRIMA

Enter **BARTELLO** and **SILVIO**.

SILVIO
Tis true she is a right good Princess, and a just one,
And Florence when she sets, has lost a Planet.

BARTELLO
My Mistriss? I tell thee gentle Nephew,
There is not such another friend to goodness,
To down-right dealing, to faith and true heart
Within the Christian confines: Before she blest us,
Justice was a Cheese-monger, a meer Cheese-monger,
Weigh'd nothing to the world but Mites and Maggots,
And a main stink: Law like a Horse-courser,
Her rules, and precepts hung with gawdes and ribbonds
And pamper'd up to cousen him that bought her,
When she her self was hackney, lame, and founder'd.

SILVIO
But the sweet Lady,
Belvidere the bright one—

BARTELLO
I, there's a face indeed: Oh my dear Nephew,
Could a young fellow of thy fiery mettle
Freeze, and that Lady in his Arms?

SILVIO
I think not.

BARTELLO
Thou hast a parlous judgement; but let that pass,
She is as truly virtuous, fair, and noble,

As her great Mother's good: and that's not ordinary.

SILVIO
But why (so many Princes, and so great ones
Being Suitors) should the Dutchess deny to match her?

BARTELLO
She is a Jewel man, hangs in her bosom,
Her only Child: with her eies she sees all things,
Discourses with her tongue, and pluck her from her
(So dotingly the old one loves her young one)
You pluck her heart out too: Besides, of late daies,
The Duke of Milan, who could never win her
By Love, nor Treaty, laid a close train for her
In her own private Walks: some forty Horse-men,
So to surprize her; which we found, and dealt with,
And sent 'em running home to the Duke their Master,
Like Dogs with bottles at their tails.

SILVIO
Since that, I heard Sir,
She has sent her to your Cittadel to secure her,
My cosin Rodope, your wife attending her.

BARTELLO
You hear a truth, and all convenient pleasures
Are there proportion'd for her.

SILVIO
I would fain, Sir,
Like one that owes a dutious service to her
Sometimes so please you—

BARTELLO
Gentle Cosin pardon me,
I must not, nor you must not dare to offer,
The last Edict lies on his life pursues it;
Your friend, Sir, to command, abroad to love you
To lend ye any thing I have, to wait upon ye,
But in the Cittadel where I stand charg'd,
Not a bit upon a march: no service, Sir,
No, good Sir by no means: I kiss your hands, Sir.

[Exit.

SILVIO
To your keeping only? none else to look upon her?
None but Bartello worthy her attendance?

No faith but his to serve her? Oh Belvidere,
Thou Saint to whom my youth is sacrific'd,
Thou point to which my life turns, and my fortune,
Art thou lock'd from me now? from all my comforts,
Art thou snatch'd violently? thou hear'st me not,
Nor canst thou see (fair soul) thy servants mournings,
Yet let thy gentle heart feel what his absence,
The great divorse of minds so truly loving,
So long, and nurs'd in one affection
Even from our infant eyes, suck'd in and nourish'd:
Oh let it feel but that, and there stand constant
And I am blest. My dear Aunt Rodope,
That is her Governess, did love me dearly,
There's one hope yet to see her: when he is absent
It may be ventur'd, and she may work it closely:
I know the Ladies will goe equal with me,
And so the danger of the Edict avoided;
Let me think more, for I must try all hazards.

[Enter **CLAUDIO** and **SOTO**.

SOTO
Will ye go yonder, Sir?

CLAUDIO
Yes marry will I Sir.

SOTO
And by this Ladder?

CLAUDIO
By that Ladder, coxcombe.

SOTO
Have ye any more necks at home when this is broken,
For this will crack with the best friend he has Sir?
Or can you pitch of all four, like an Ape now?
Let me see you tumble.

CLAUDIO
You are very pleasant Sir.

SOTO
No truly Sir, I should be loath to see ye
Come fluttering down like a young Rook, cry squab,
And take ye up with your brains beaten into your buttocks.

CLAUDIO

Hold your peace Asse: who's this stands musing here?
Sylvio?

SILVIO
Who calls me?

CLAUDIO
One most glad to see you Sir.

SILVIO
My dearest Claudio? what make you thus private,
And with a preparation of this nature?

SOTO
We have leave to play, and are going to climb Birds nests.

SILVIO
Prethee what is it friend? why start ye from me?
Is your old Mistriss grown so coy and cruel,
She must be scal'd? it seems you are loath to tell me,
Since twenty years continuance of our friendship
May not be worth the weight of such a secret,
'Twill be but rude to aske again: save ye.

CLAUDIO
Nay stay, dear Silvio, if you love me take it:
For till you know it, never woman labour'd
As I do now.

SILVIO
I'll doe my best to ease it.

CLAUDIO
You have heard the Lady Belvidere—

SILVIO
What heard Sir?

CLAUDIO
Heard to the Cittadel, upon some fears
She is confin'd.

SILVIO
Why dreams he on this beauty?
'Tis true, I have heard it.

CLAUDIO
And that no access,

No blessing from those eyes, but with much hazard,
Even hazard of a life.

SILVIO
He dares not love her;
I have heard that too: but whither points your purpose?

CLAUDIO
Oh Silvio, let me speak that none may hear me,
None but thy truth: I have lov'd this Lady long,
Long given away my life to her devotion,
Long dwelt upon that beauty to my ruine.

SILVIO
Do's she know this?

CLAUDIO
No, there begins my misery,
Ixion-like, I have only yet clasp'd clouds,
And fed upon poor empty dreams that starve me.

SILVIO
And what do you mean to do now?

CLAUDIO
Though I dye for't.
Though all the tortures in the world hung on me,
Arm'd with imperious Love, I stand prepar'd now,
With this to reach her Chamber: there to see her,
And tell her boldly with what truth I love her.

SILVIO
'Twill not be easily done Sir.

CLAUDIO
Oh my Silvio,
The hardest things are sweetest in possession.

SILVIO
Nor will shew much discretion.

CLAUDIO
Love is blind man,
And he that looks for reason there far blinder.

SILVIO
Have ye consider'd ripely?

CLAUDIO
All that may fall,
And arm'd against that all.

SILVIO
Her honor too?
What she may suffer in this rash adventure
The beauty of her name?

CLAUDIO
I'll doe it closely,
And only at her window, with that caution—

SILVIO
Are there no Guards?

CLAUDIO
Corruption chokes their service.

SILVIO
Or do you hold her bred so light a woman
To hold commerce with strange tongues?

CLAUDIO
Why this service,
This only hazard of my life must tell her,
Though she were Vestas self, I must deserve her.

SILVIO
I would not have ye go: pray let it sink here,
And think a nobler way to raise your service,
A safer and a wiser.

CLAUDIO
'Tis too late, Sir.

SILVIO
Then I must say, You shall not goe.

CLAUDIO
I shall not?

SILVIO
You shall not go: that part bred with ye, friendship
Bids me say boldly so, and you observe me.

CLAUDIO
You stretch that tye too far.

SILVIO
I'll stretch it farther:
The honor that I bear that spotless virtue
You fouly seek to taint, unnobly covet,
Bids me command ye stay: if not, thus force ye.

SOTO
This will be worse than climbing.

CLAUDIO
Why do ye draw Sir?

SILVIO
To kill thee, if thy base will be thy Master.

CLAUDIO
I ever was your friend.

SILVIO
Whilst thou wert honest,
And not a Night-thief of anothers honor;
I never call'd a fool my friend, a mad man,
That durst expose his fame to all opinions,
His life to unhonest dangers: I never lov'd him,
Durst know his name, that sought a Virgins ruine,
Nor ever took I pleasure in acquaintance
With men, that give as loose rains to their fancies
As the wild Ocean to his raging fluxes:
A noble soul I twin with, and my love
Followes his life, dares master his affections.
Will ye give off, or fight?

CLAUDIO
I will not fight with ye:
The sacred name of friend ties up that anger,
Rather I'll study.

SILVIO
Do, to be a friend still.

CLAUDIO
If this way, I shall never hold.

SILVIO
I'll watch ye:
And if I catch ye false: by heaven ye dye for't,
All love forgot.

CLAUDIO
When I fear that, I am fit for't.

[Exeunt.

SCÆNA SECUNDA

Enter **LOPEZ** at a Table with Jewels and Money upon it, an Egg roasting by a Candle.

LOPEZ
Whilst prodigal young gaudy fools are banqueting,
And launching out their states to catch the giddy,
Thus do I study to preserve my fortune,
And hatch with care at home the wealth that Saints me.
Here's Rubies of Bengala, rich, rich, glorious;
These Diamonds of Ormus bought for little,
Here vented at the price of Princes Ransomes;
How bright they shine like constellations,
The South Seas treasure here, Pearl, fair and orient
Able to equal Cleopatra's Banquet:
Here chains of lesser stones for Ladies lusters,
Ingotts of Gold, Rings, Brooches, bars of Silver,
These are my studies to set off in sale well,
And not in sensual surfeits to consume 'em;
How rosts mine egg; he heats apace, I'll turn him:
Penurio, where you knave do you wait? Penurio,
You lazie knave.

PENURIO
Did you call Sir?

LOPEZ
Where's your Mistriss?
What vanity holds her from her attendance?

PENURIO
The very sight of this egg has made him cockish,
What would a dozen butter'd do? She is within Sir.

LOPEZ
Within Sir, at what thrift ye knave? what getting?

PENURIO
Getting a good stomach Sir, and she knew where to get meat to it,
She is praying heartily upon her knees Sir,

That Heaven would send her a good bearing dinner.

LOPEZ
Nothing but gluttony and surfeit thought on,
Health flung behind: had she not yesternight sirrah
Two Sprats to supper, and the oil allowable?
Was she not sick with eating? Hadst not thou,
(Thou most ungrateful knave, that nothing satisfies)
The water that I boil'd my other egg in
To make thee hearty broth?

PENURIO
'Tis true, I had Sir;
But I might as soon make the Philosophers Stone on't,
You gave it me in water, and but for manners sake,
I could give it you again, in wind, it was so hearty
I shall turn pissing-Conduit shortly: my Mistriss comes, Sir.

[Enter **ISABELLA**.

LOPEZ
Welcome my Dove.

ISABELLA
Pray ye keep your welcome to ye,
Unless it carries more than words to please me,
Is this the joy to be a Wife? to bring with me,
Besides the nobleness of blood I spring from,
A full and able portion to maintain me?
Is this the happiness of youth and beauty,
The great content of being made a Mistriss,
To live a Slave subject to wants and hungers,
To jealousies for every eye that wanders?
Unmanly jealousie.

LOPEZ
Good Isabella.

ISABELLA
Too good for you: do you think to famish me,
Or keep me like an Alms-woman in such rayment,
Such poor unhandsome weeds? am I old, or ugly?
I never was bred thus: and if your misery
Will suffer wilful blindness to abuse me,
My patience shall be no Bawd to mine own ruine.

PENURIO
Tickle him Mistris: to him.

ISABELLA
Had ye love in ye,
Or any part of man—

PENURIO
Follow that Mistriss.

ISABELLA
Or had humanity but ever known ye,
You would shame to use a woman of my way thus,
So poor, and basely; you are strangely jealous of me
If I should give ye cause.

LOPEZ
How Isabella?

ISABELLA
As do not venture this way to provoke me.

PENURIO
Excellent well Mistriss.

LOPEZ
How's this Isabella?

ISABELLA
'Twill stir a Saint, and I am but a woman,
And by that tenure may—

LOPEZ
By no means chicken,
You know I love ye: fie, take no example
By those young gadding Dames: (you are noted virtuous)
That stick their Husbands wealth in trifles on 'em
And point 'em but the way to their own miseries:
I am not jealous, kiss me,—I am not:
And for your Diet, 'tis to keep you healthful,
Surfeits destroy more than the sword: that I am careful
Your meat should be both neat, and cleanly handled
See, Sweet, I am Cook my self, and mine own Cater.

PENURIO
A—of that Cook cannot lick his fingers.

LOPEZ
I'll add another dish: you shall have Milk to it,
'Tis nourishing and good.

PENURIO
With Butter in't Sir?

LOPEZ
This knave would breed a famine in a Kingdom:
And cloths that shall content ye: you must be wise then,
And live sequestred to your self and me,
Not wandring after every toy comes cross ye,
Nor struck with every spleen: what's the knave doing? Penurio.

PENURIO
Hunting Sir, for a second course of Flies here,
They are rare new Sallads.

LOPEZ
For certain Isabella
This ravening fellow has a Wolf in's belly:
Untemperate knave, will nothing quench thy appetite?
I saw him eat two Apples, which is monstrous.

PENURIO
If you had given me those 't had been more monstrous.

LOPEZ
'Tis a main miracle to feed this villain,
Come Isabella, let us in to supper,
And think the Roman dainties at our Table,
'Tis all but thought.

[Exeunt.

PENURIO
Would all my thoughts would do it:
The Devil should think of purchasing that Egg-shell,
To victual out a Witch for the Burmoothes:
'Tis Treason to any good stomach living now
To hear a tedious Grace said, and no meat to't,
I have a Radish yet, but that's but transitory.

[Exit.

SCÆNA TERTIA

Enter **SOTO**.

SOTO

Can any living man, unless a Rascal
That neither knows himself, nor a fashion'd Gentleman
Take me for a worse man than my Master now?
I am naturally proud in these clothes: but if pride now
Should catch a fall in what I am attempting,
'Tis but a Proverb sound, and a neck broken,
That's the worst can come on't, a Gentleman's gone then,
A Gentleman o'th' first house, there's the end on't:
My Master lies most pittifully complaining,
Wringing and kicking up to th' ears in love yonder,
And such a lamentable noise he keeps, it kills me:
I have got his cloaths, and if I can get to her
By hook or crook here, such a song I'll sing her—
I think I shall be hang'd, but that's no matter,
What's a hanging among friends: I am valiant now as an Elephant,
I have consider'd what to say too: let me see now,
This is the place, 'tis plaguy high: stay at that lower window
Let me aim finely now, like a good Gunner,
It may prove but a whipping.

[Enter **SILVIO**.

SILVIO

I saw some body
Pass by me now, and though it were dark, me-thought yet
I knew the clothes: ha, let me not be cozen'd,
The Ladder too, ready to fling it? monstrous,
'Tis he, 'tis Claudio: most voluptuous villain,
Scandal to womans credit: Love, I forget thee.

SOTO

What will he do i'th' name of Heaven, what's that there?

SILVIO

And all the friendship that I bore thee, bury here.

SOTO

What has he in's hand? I hope but a Cudgel.

SILVIO

Thy faul'ts forgive O Heaven: farewel thou traitor.

SOTO

I am slain: I am slain.

SILVIO

He's down, and dead: dead certain,

'Twas too rash, too full of spleen, stark dead:
This is no place now to repent in, only
Would I had given this hand that shot the Pistol
I had miss'd thee, and thou wer't once more Claudio.

[Exit.

[Enter **CLAUDIO**.

CLAUDIO
Why should I love thus foolishly? thus desperately?
And give away my heart where no hope's left me?
Why should not the true counsel of a friend restrain me?
The Devils mouth I run into affright me,
The honor of the Lady, charm my wildness;
I have no power, no Being of my self,
No reason strong enough now left within me
To bind my Will: Oh Love, thou god, or devil,
Or what thou art, that playes the tyrant in me.

SOTO
Oh.

CLAUDIO
What's that cry?

SOTO
A Surgeon, a Surgeon,
Twenty good Surgeons.

CLAUDIO
'Tis not far from me,
Some murther o' my life.

SOTO
Will you let me dye here?
No drink come, nor no Surgeon?

CLAUDIO
'Tis my man sure,
His voice, and here he lies: how is it with thee?

SOTO
I am slain, Sir, I am slain.

CLAUDIO
Slain? Who has slain thee?

SOTO
Kill'd, kill'd, out-right kill'd.

CLAUDIO
Where's thy hurt?

SOTO
I know not,
But I am sure I am kill'd.

CLAUDIO
Canst thou sit up,
That I may find the hurt out?

SOTO
I can sit up,
But ne'er the less I am slain.

CLAUDIO
'Tis not o' this side?

SOTO
No Sir, I think it be not.

CLAUDIO
Nor o' this side,
Was it done with a sword?

SOTO
A Gun, a Gun, sweet Master.

CLAUDIO
The devil a bullet has been here: thou art well man.

SOTO
No sure I am kill'd.

CLAUDIO
Let me see thy thighs, and belly,
As whole as a fish for any thing I see yet:
Thou bleed'st no where.

SOTO
I think I do not bleed, Sir,
But yet I am afraid I am slain.

CLAUDIO
Stand up fool,

Thou hast as much hurt as my nail; who shot thee,
A Pottle, or a Pint?

SOTO
Signior Silvio shot me
In these clothes; taking me for you, and seeing
The Ladder in my hand here, which I stole from ye,
Thinking to have gone to the Lady my self, and have spoke for ye.

CLAUDIO
If he had hit ye home, he had serv'd ye right sirrah,
You saucy rogue, how poor my intent shews to me,
How naked now, and foolish!

SOTO
Are ye sure he has not hit me,
It gave a monstrous bounce?

CLAUDIO
You rose o' your right side,
And said your prayers too, you had been payed else:
But what need'st thou a Bullet, when thy fear kills thee?
Sirrah, keep your own counsel for all this, you'll be hang'd else,
If it be known.

SOTO
If it be by my means, let me;
I am glad I am not kill'd, and far more gladder
My Gentleman-like humor's out: I feel 'tis dangerous,
And to be a gentleman, is to be kill'd twice a week.

CLAUDIO
Keep your self close i'th' Countrey for a while sirrah.
There's Money, walk to your friends.

SOTO
They have no Pistols,
Nor are no Gentlemen, that's my comfort.

[Exit.

CLAUDIO
I will retire too, and live private; for this Silvio,
Inflam'd with nobleness, will be my death else;
And if I can forget this love that loads me,
At least the danger: and now I think on't better,
I have some conclusions else invites me to it.

[Exit.

Enter **RODOPE**, and **SILVIO** at several doors.

RODOPE
Nephew.

SILVIO
My dear Aunt.

RODOPE
Would you go by thus slily,
And never see me, not once send in to me
Your loving Aunt? she that above all those
I call my kindred, honour'd you, and placed you
Nearest my heart?

SILVIO
I thank you worthy Aunt
But such at this time are my occasions—

RODOPE
You shall not goe yet, by my faith you shall not,
I will not be deny'd: why look ye sad Nephew?

SILVIO
I am seldom other: Oh, this blood sits heavy:
As I walk'd this way late last night,
In meditation of some things concern'd me—

RODOPE
What Nephew?

SILVIO
Why methought I heard a Piece, Lady,
A Piece shot off, much about this place too,
But could not judge the cause, nor what it boaded,
Under the Castle-wall.

RODOPE
We heard it too,
And the Watch pursu'd it presently, but found nothing,

Not any tract.

SILVIO
I am right glad to hear it:
The Ruffians surely that command the night
Have found him, stript him: and into the River
Convey'd the body.

RODOPE
You look still sadder, Nephew,
Is any thing within these walls to comfort ye?
Speak, and be Master of it.

SILVIO
Ye are a right Courtier,
A great Professor, but a poor performer.

RODOPE
Do you doubt my faith: you never found me that way.
I dare well speak it boldly, but a true friend.

SILVIO
Continue then.

RODOPE
Try me, and see who falters.

SILVIO
I will, and presently: 'tis in your power
To make me the most bound man to your courtesie.

RODOPE
Let me know how, and if I fail—

SILVIO
'Tis thus then,
Get me access to the Lady Belvidere,
But for a minute, but to see her: your Husband now
Is safe at Court, I left him full employ'd there.

RODOPE
You have ask'd the thing without my power to grant ye,
The Law lies on the danger: if I lov'd ye not
I would bid ye goe, and there be found, and dye for't.

SILVIO
I knew your love, and where there shew'd a danger
How far you durst step for me: give me a true friend;

That where occasion is to do a benefit
Aims at the end, and not the rubs before it;
I was a fool to ask ye this, a more fool
To think a woman had so much noble nature
To entertain a secret of this burthen;
Ye had best to tell the Dutchess I perswaded ye,
That's a fine course, and one will win ye credit;
Forget the name of Cosin, blot my blood out,
And so you raise your self, let me grow shorter.
A woman friend? he that believes that weakness
Steers in a stormy night without a Compass.

RODOPE
What is't I durst not do might not impeach ye?

SILVIO
Why this ye dare not do, ye dare not think of.

RODOPE
'Tis a main hazard.

SILVIO
If it were not so
I would not come to you to seek a favour.

RODOPE
You will lose your self.

SILVIO
The loss ends with my self then.

RODOPE
You will but see her?

SILVIO
Only look upon her.

RODOPE
Not stay?

SILVIO
Prescribe your time.

RODOPE
Not traffique with her
In any close dishonourable action?

SILVIO

Stand you your self by.

RODOPE
I will venture for ye,
Because ye shall be sure I am a touch'd friend,
I'll bring her to ye: come walk, you know the Garden,
And take this key to open the little Postern,
There stand no guards.

SILVIO
I shall soon find it Aunt.

[Exeunt.

SCÆNA SECUNDA

Enter two **SOLDIERS**.

1ST SOLDIER
Is the Captain come home?

2ND SOLDIER
No, who commands the Guard to night?

1ST SOLDIER
I think Petruchio.

2ND SOLDIER
What's the Word?

1ST SOLDIER
None knows yet.

2ND SOLDIER
I would this Lady were married out o'th'way once,
Or out of our custodies; I wish they would take in more companies,
For I am sure we feel her in our duties shrewdly.

1ST SOLDIER
'Tis not her fault I warrant ye, she is ready for't,
And that's the plague, when they grow ripe for marriage
They must be slipt like Hawkes.

2ND SOLDIER
Give me a mean wench,
No State doubt lies on her, she is alwayes ready.

1ˢᵀ SOLDIER
Come to the Guard, 'tis late, and sure the Captain
Can not be long away.

2ᴺᴰ SOLDIER
I have watch'd these three nights,
To morrow they may keep me tame for nothing.

[Exeunt.

SCÆNA TERTIA

Enter **SILVIO**, **BELVIDERE**, and **RODOPE** with a Light.

SILVIO
This is the place I think; what Light is that there?
The Lady and my Cosin?

BELVIDERE
Is this the Garden?

RODOPE
Yes Madam.

SILVIO
Oh my blessed Mistriss,
Saint of my soul.

BELVIDERE
Speak softly: take me to ye,
Oh Silvio, I am thine, thine ever Silvio.

RODOPE
Is this your promise, Sir? Lady your honor?
I am undone if this be seen, disgrac'd,
Fallen under all discredit.

BELVIDERE
Do you love still?
Dear, do you keep your old faith?

SILVIO
Ever Lady;
And when that fails me, all that's good forsake me.

RODOPE
Do not you shame? Madam, I must not suffer this,
I will not suffer it; men call you virtuous,
What do you mean to lose your self thus; Silvio?
I charge thee get away, I charge you retire ye,
I'll call the Watch else.

SILVIO
Call all the world to see us,
We live in one anothers happiness,
And so will die.

BELVIDERE
Here will I hang for ever.

RODOPE
As ye respect me, as hereafter Madam
You would enjoy his love—nothing prevail with ye?
I'll try my strength then; get thee gone thou villain,
Thou Promise-breaker.

SILVIO
I am tide, I cannot.

RODOPE
I'll ring the Bell then.

SILVIO
Ring it to death, I am fixt here.

[Enter **BARTELLO**, two **SOLDIERS** with lights.

BARTELLO
I saw a Light over the Garden walk,
Hard by the Ladies Chamber, here's some knavery
As I live, I saw it twice.

RODOPE
The Guard, the Guard there;
I must not suffer this, it is too mischievous.

BARTELLO
Light up the Torch, I fear'd this, ha? young Silvio?
How got he in?

1ST SOLDIER
The Devil brought him in sure
He came not by us.

BARTELLO

My wife between 'em busling?
Guard, pull him off.

RODOPE

Now, now, ye feel the misery.

BARTELLO

You, Madam, at an hour so far undecent?
Death, O my soul! this is a foul fault in ye,
Your mothers care abus'd too, Light's to her Chamber,
I am sorry to see this.

BELVIDERE

Farewel my Silvio,
And let no danger sink thee.

SILVIO

Nor death Lady.

[Exeunt **BELVIDERE, RODOPE.**

BARTELLO

Are ye so hot? I shall prepare ye Physick
Will purge ye finely, neatly: you are too fiery,
Think of your prayers, Sir, an you have not forgot 'em;
Can ye flie i' th' air, or creep ye in at key-holes?
I have a Gin will catch ye though you conjur'd:
Take him to Guard to night, to strong and sure Guard;
I'll back to th' Dutchess presently: no less sport serve ye,
Than the Heir to a Dukedom? play at push-pin there Sir?
It was well aim'd, but plague upon't, you shot short,
And that will lose your game.

SILVIO

I know the loss then.

[Exeunt.

SCÆNA QUARTA

Enter **CLAUDIO** like a Merchant.

CLAUDIO

Now, in this habit may I safely see

How my incensed friend carries my murther,
Who little I imagin'd had been wrought
To such a height of rage, and much I grieve now
Mine own blind passion had so master'd me,
I could not see his love, for sure he loves her,
And on a nobler ground than I pretended.

[Enter **PENURIO**.

It must be so, it is so; what Penurio,
My shotten friend, what wind blew you?

PENURIO
Faith 'tis true,
Any strong wind will blow me like a Feather,
I am all Air, nothing of earth within me,
Nor have not had this month, but that good Dinner
Your Worship gave me yesterday, that staies by me,
And gives me ballast, else the Sun would draw me.

CLAUDIO
But does my Mistriss speak still of me?

PENURIO
Yes, Sir,
And in her sleep, that makes my Master mad too,
And turn and fart for anger.

CLAUDIO
Art sure she saw me?

PENURIO
She saw ye at a window.

CLAUDIO
'Tis most true,
In such a place I saw a Gentlewoman,
A young, sweet, handsome woman.

PENURIO
That's she, that's she Sir.

CLAUDIO
And well she view'd me, I view'd her.

PENURIO
Still she Sir.

CLAUDIO
At last she blush'd, and then look'd off.

PENURIO
That blush, Sir,
If you can read it truly—

CLAUDIO
But didst thou tell her,
Or didst thou fool me, thou knew'st such a one?

PENURIO
I told her, and I told her such a sweet tale—

CLAUDIO
But did she hear thee?

PENURIO
With a thousand ears, Sir,
And swallow'd what I said as greedily,
As great-belly'd women do Cherries, stones and all Sir.

CLAUDIO
Methinks she should not love thy Master?

PENURIO
Hang him Pilcher,
There's nothing loves him: his own Cat cannot endure him,
She had better lye with a Bear, for he is so hairy,
That a tame Warren of Fleas frisk round about him.

CLAUDIO
And wilt thou work still?

PENURIO
Like a Miner for ye.

CLAUDIO
And get access.

PENURIO
Or conjure you together,
'Tis her desire to meet: she is poyson'd with him,
And till she take a sweet fresh air, that's you Sir.

CLAUDIO
There's money for thee: thou art a precious Varlet
Be fat, be fat, and blow thy Master backward.

PENURIO

Blow you my Mistriss, Sir, as flat as a Flounder,
Then blow her up again, as Butchers blow their Veals;
If she dye upon the same
Bury her, bury her in Gods name.

CLAUDIO

Thou art a merry knave: by this hand I'll feed thee,
Till thou crack'st at both ends, if thou dar'st do this
Thou shall eat no fantastical Porridge,
Nor lick the dish where oil was yesterday,
Dust, and dead Flies to day; Capons, fat Capons—

PENURIO

Oh hearty sound.

CLAUDIO

Cramb'd full of itching Oysters.

PENURIO

Will ye have the Dutchess?

CLAUDIO

And Lobsters big as Gauntlets,
Thou shalt despise base Beef.

PENURIO

I do despise it,
And now methinks I feel a Tart come sliding.

CLAUDIO

Leaping into thy mouth: but first deal faithfully.

PENURIO

When will ye come?

CLAUDIO

To morrow.

PENURIO

I'll attend ye,
For then my Master will be out in business.

CLAUDIO

What news abroad?

PENURIO

'Mas, as I was coming to you,
I heard that Signior Silvio, a good Gentleman,
Many a good meal I have eaten with him—

CLAUDIO
What of him?

PENURIO
Was this day to be arraigned before the Dutchess,
But why, I could not hear.

CLAUDIO
Silvio arraign'd?
Go, get ye gone, and think of me.

PENURIO
I flie Sir.

[Exit **PENURIO**.

CLAUDIO
Arraign'd? for what? for my supposed death? no,
That cannot be sure, there's no rumor of it,
Be it what it will, I will be there and see it,
And if my help will bring him off, he has it.

[Exit.

SCÆNA QUINTA

Enter **DUCHESS**, **LORDS**, **SILVIO** prisoner, **BELVIDERE**, **BARTELLO**, **RODOPE**, **CLERK**, **COUNSELLORS**, **ATTENDANTS**.

DUCHESS
Read the Edict last made,
Keep silence there.

CLERK
If any man of what condition soever, and a subject,
after the publishing of this Edict, shall without special
Licence from the great Dutchess, attempt or buy, offer,
or make an attempt, to solicite the love of the Princess
Belvidere, the person so offending, shall forfeit his life.

COUNSELLOR
The reason why my Royal Mistriss here
In her last Treaty with Siennas Duke,

Promis'd her beauteous daughter there in marriage,
The Duke of Milan, rival in this fortune,
Un-nobly sought by practice to betray her;
Which found, and cross'd, the Cittadel receiv'd her
There to secure her Mothers word; the last cause
So many Gentlemen of late enamour'd
On this most beauteous Princess, and not brooking
One more than other, to deserve a favour,
Bloud has been spilt, many brave spirits lost,
And more, unless she had been kept, close from their violence,
Had like to have followed: therefore for due prevention
Of all such hazards and unnoble actions,
This last Edict was published, which thou Silvio
Like a false man, a bad man, and a Traitor
Hast rent a-peeces, and contemn'd, for which cause
Thou standest a guilty man here now.

[Enter **CLAUDIO**.

CLERK
Speak Silvio,
What canst thou say to avoid the hand of Justice?

SILVIO
Nothing, but I confess, submit and lay my head to it.

BELVIDERE
Have ye no eyes my Lords, no understandings?
The Gentleman will cast himself away,
Cast himself wilfully: are you, or you guilty?
No more is he, no more taint sticks upon him:
I drew him thither; 'twas my way betrai'd him,
I got the entrance kept, I entertain'd him,
I hid the danger from him, forced him to me,
Poor gentle soul, he's in no part transgressing,
I wrote unto him.

SILVIO
Do not wrong that honor,
Cast not upon that pureness these aspersions,
By Heaven it was my love, my violence,
My life must answer it: I broke in to her,
Tempted the Law, solicited unjustly.

BELVIDERE
As there is truth in Heaven, I was the first cause:
How could this man have come to me, left naked
Without my counsel and provision?

What hour could he find out to pass the Watches,
But I must make it sure first? Reverend Judges,
Be not abus'd, nor let an innocent life lie
Upon your shaking Conscience; I did it,
My love the main wheel that set him a going:
His motion but compell'd.

SILVIO
Can ye believe this?
And know with what a modesty and whiteness
Her life was ever ranck'd? Can you believe this
And see me here before ye, young and wilful?
Apt to what danger Love dares thrust me on,
And where Law stops my way, apt to contemn it?
If I were bashful, old, or dull, and sleepy
In Loves allarms, a woman might awake me,
Direct, and clew me out the way to happiness:
But I, like fire, kindled with that bright beauty,
Catch hold of all occasions, and run through 'em.

BELVIDERE
I charge ye, as your honest souls will answer it.

SILVIO
I charge ye, as you are the friends to virtue,
That has no pattern living but this Lady.

BELVIDERE
Let not his blood—

SILVIO
Let not her wilfulness—
For then you act a Scene Hell will rejoyce at.

BELVIDERE
He is clear.

SILVIO
She is as white in this as Infants.

CLAUDIO
The god of Love protect your cause, and help ye,
Two nobler pieces of affection
These eyes ne'er look'd on, if such goodness perish,
Let never true hearts meet again, but break.

[Exit.

1ST LORD
A strange exemple of strong love, a rare one.

2ND LORD
Madam, we know not what to say, to think on.

DUCHESS
I must confess it strikes me tender too,
Searches my Mothers heart: you found 'em there?

BARTELLO
Yes certain Madam.

DUCHESS
And so linked together?

BARTELLO
As they had been one piece of Alablaster.

DUCHESS
Nothing dishonourable?

SILVIO
So let my soul have happiness,
As that thought yet durst never seek this bosom.

DUCHESS
What shall I do? 'has broke my Law, abus'd me,
Fain would I know the truth, either confess it,
And let me understand the main offender,
Or both shall feel the torture.

SILVIO
Are ye a Mother;
The Mother of so sweet a Rose as this is?
So pure a Flower? and dare ye lose that nature?
Dare ye take to your self so great a wickedness,
(Oh holy Heaven) of thinking what may ruine
This goodly building? this Temple where the gods dwell?
Give me a thousand tortures, I deserve 'em,
And shew me death in all the shapes imagin'd.

BELVIDERE
No death but I will answer it, meet it, seek it;
No torture but I'll laugh upon't, and kiss it.

1ST LORD
This is no way.

2ND LORD

They say no more for certain
Than their strong hearts will suffer.

DUCHESS

I have bethought me;
No Lords, although I have a Child offending,
Nature dares not forget she is a Child still;
Till now, I never look'd on love imperious:
I have bethought me of a way to break ye,
To separate, though not your loves, your bodies:
Silvio attend, I'll be your Judge my self now,
The sentence of your death (because my Daughter
Will bear an equal part in your afflictions)
I take away and pardon: this remains then
An easie and a gentle punishment,
And this shall be fulfill'd: because unnobly
You have sought the love, and marriage of a Princess,
The absolute and sole Heir of this Dukedom,
By that means, as we must imagine strongly,
To plant your self into this rule hereafter,
We here pronounce ye a man banish'd from us.

SILVIO

For ever banish'd Lady?

DUCHESS

Yet more mercy,
But for a year: and then again in this place
To make your full appearance: yet more pitty,
If in that time you can absolve a question,
Writ down within this scrowl, absolve it rightly,
This Lady is your wife, and shall live with ye;
If not, you loose your head.

SILVIO

I take this honor,
And humbly kiss those Royal hands.

DUCHESS

Receive it: Bartello, to your old guard take the Princess,
And so the Court break up.

SILVIO

Farewel to all,
And to that spotless heart my endless service.

[Exit.

1ST LORD
What will this prove?

2ND LORD
I'll tell you a year hence, Sir.

[Exeunt.

[Enter **PENURIO, ISABELLA, CLAUDIO.**

PENURIO
Are you pleas'd now? have not I wrought this wonder
Non eben fatto Signieur.

CLAUDIO
Rarely Penurio.

PENURIO
Close, close then, and work wax.

CLAUDIO
I am studying for thee
A dinner, that shall victual thee for ten year.

PENURIO
Do you hear Mistriss?
You know what a dundir whelp my Master is,
I need not preach to ye, how unfit and wanting
To give a woman satisfaction:
How he stinks, and snores, a Bull's a better bed-fellow;
And for his love, never let that deceive ye.

ISABELLA
Nay sure he loves me not.

PENURIO
If he could coyn ye,
Or turn ye into mettal, much might be then;
He loves not any thing but what is traffique:
I have heard him swear he would sell ye to the Grand Signior.

ISABELLA

The Turk?

PENURIO
The very Turk, and how they would use ye.

ISABELLA
I'll fit him for't: the Turk?

PENURIO
I know the price too:
Now ye have time to pay him, pay him home Mistriss;
Pay him o' th' pate, clout him for all his courtesies;
Here's one that dances in your eyes, young delicate
To work this vengeance; if ye let it slip now,
There is no pittying of ye, od's precious, Mistriss,
Were I his wife, I would so mall his Mazard,
'Tis charity, meer charity, pure charity,
Are you the first? has it not been from Eves time,
Women would have their safe revenges this way?
And good and gracious women, excellent women;
Is't not a handsome Gentleman? a sweet Gentleman;
View him from head to foot, a compleat Gentleman;
When can ye hope the like again? I leave ye,
And my revenge too, with ye; I know my office,
I'll not be far off, be not long a fumbling,
When danger shall appear, I'll give the 'larme.

[Exit.

ISABELLA
You are welcome, Sir, and would it were my fortune
To afford a Gentleman of your fair seeming,
A freer entertainment than this house has,
You partly know, Sir.—

CLAUDIO
Know, and pity Lady,
Such sweetness in the bud, should be so blasted;
Dare you make me your Servant?

ISABELLA
Dare you make Sir,
That service worthy of a womans favour
By constancy and goodness?

CLAUDIO
Here I swear to ye,
By the unvalued love I bear this beauty,

(And kiss the Book too) never to be recreant,
To honour ye, to truly love, and serve ye,
My youth to wait upon ye, what my wealth has.

ISABELLA
Oh make me not so poor to sell affection,
Those bought loves Sir, wear faster than the moneys;
A handsome Gentleman.

CLAUDIO
A most delicate sweet one,
Let my truth purchase then.

ISABELLA
I should first try it,
But you may happily.—

CLAUDIO
You shall not doubt me,
I hope she loves me; when I prove false, shame take me;
Will ye believe a little?

ISABELLA
I fear, too much, Sir.

CLAUDIO
And will ye love a little?

ISABELLA
That should be your part:

CLAUDIO
Thus I begin then, thus and thus.

ISABELLA
A good beginning,
We have a proverb saies, makes a good ending.

CLAUDIO
Say ye so? 'tis well inferr'd.

ISABELLA
Good Sir, your patience:
Methinks I have ventur'd now, like a weak Bark
Upon a broken billow, that will swallow me,
Upon a rough Sea of suspitions,
Stuck round with jealous rocks.

PENURIO
within. A hem, a hem there.

ISABELLA
This is my man; my fears too soon have found me,

[Enter **PENURIO**.

Now what's the news?

PENURIO
A pox of yonder old Rigel,
The Captain, the old Captain.

ISABELLA
What old Captain?

PENURIO
Captain courageous yonder of the Castle,
Captain, Don Diego, old Bartello.

ISABELLA
Where is he?

PENURIO
He's coming in:
'Twould vex the Devil, that such an old Potgun as this,
That can make no sport, should hinder them that can do it.

ISABELLA
I would not have him see the Gentleman,
For all the world, my credit were undone then.

PENURIO
Shall I fling a piss-pot on's head as he comes in,
And take him into th' kitchin, there to drie him.

ISABELLA
That will not do; and he is so humorous too
He will come in.

CLAUDIO
What is he?

ISABELLA
One much troubles me.

PENURIO

And can do nothing, cannot eat.

ISABELLA
Your sight now,
Out of a driveling dotage he bears to me,
May make him tell my husband, and undo me.

CLAUDIO
What would ye have me do?

ISABELLA
But for a while Sir,
Step here behind this hanging, presently
I'll answer him, and then—

CLAUDIO
I will obey ye.

[Enter **BARTELLO**.

BARTELLO
Where's my rich Jeweller? I have stones to sett.

PENURIO
He is abroad, and sure Sir.

BARTELLO
There's for your service:
Where's the fair Lady? all alone sweet beauty?

ISABELLA
She's never much alone Sir, that's acquainted
With such companions as good honest thoughts are.

BARTELLO
I'll sit down by thee, and I'll kiss thy hand too,
And in thine ear swear by my life I love thee.

ISABELLA
Ye are a merry Captain.

BARTELLO
And a mad one, Lady;
By th' mas thou hast goodly eies, excellent eies, wench,
Ye twinkling rogues, look what thy Captain brings thee,
Thou must needs love me, love me heartily,
Hug me, and love me, hug me close.

ISABELLA
Fie Captain.

BARTELLO
Nay, I have strength, and I can strain ye sirrah,
And vault into my seat as nimbly, little one.
As any of your smooth-chinn'd boys in Florence,
I must needs commit a little folly with ye,
I'll not be long, a brideling cast, and away wench;
The hob-nail thy husband's as fitly out o'th' way now?

ISABELLA
Do you think he keeps a bawdy-house?

BARTELLO
That's all one.

ISABELLA
Or did you ever see that lightness in my carriage,
That you might promise to your self—.

BARTELLO
Away fool,
A good turn's a good turn; I am an honest fellow:

ISABELLA
You have a handsome wife, a virtuous Gentlewoman.

BARTELLO
They are not for this time o'th' year.

ISABELLA
A Lady,
That ever bore that great respect to you,
That noble constancy.

BARTELLO
That's more than I know.

[Enter **MAID** and **PENURIO**.

MAID
Oh Mistriss, ye are undone, my Master's coming.

PENURIO
Coming hard by here.

BARTELLO

Plague consume the Rascal,
Shall I make petty-patties of him?

ISABELLA
Now what love Sir?
Fear of your coming made him jealous first;
Your finding here, will make him mad and desperate,
And what in that wild mood he will execute—

BARTELLO
I can think of nothing, I have no wit left me,
Certain my head's a Mustard-pot.

ISABELLA
I have thought Sir,
And if you'll please to put in execution
What I conceive—

BARTELLO
I'll do it, tell it quickly.

ISABELLA
Draw your sword quickly, and go down inrag'd,
As if you had persu'd some foe up hither,
And grumble to your self extreamly, terribly,
But not a word to him, and so pass by him.

BARTELLO
I'll do it perfectly.

[Enter **LOPEZ**.

ISABELLA
Stand you still good Sir.

BARTELLO
Rascal, slave, villain, take a house so poorly,
After thou hast wrong'd a Gentleman, a Soldier,
Base Poultroon boy, you will forsake your neast sirrah.

LOPEZ
The matter, good sweet Captain?

BARTELLO
Run-away rogue,
And take a house to cover thy base cowardize,
I'll whip ye, I'll so scourge ye.

[Exit.

LOPEZ
Mercy upon me,
What's all this matter wife?

ISABELLA
Did you meet the mad man?

LOPEZ
I never saw the Captain so provok'd yet.

ISABELLA
Oh he's a Devil sure, a most bloody devil,
He follow'd a young Gentleman, his sword drawn,
With such a fury, how I shake to think on't,
And foyn'd, and slash'd at him, and swore he'd kill him,
Drove him up hither, follow'd him still bloodily,
And if I had not hid him, sure had slain him;
A merciless old man.

CLAUDIO
Most virtuous Lady,
Even as the giver of my life, I thank ye.

LOPEZ
This fellow must not stay here, he is too handsome;
He is gone Sir, and you may pass now with all security,
I'll be your guide my self, and such a way
I'll lead ye, none shall cross, nor none shall know ye.
The door's left open Sirrah, I'll starve you for this trick,
I'll make thee fast o' Sundaies; and for you Lady,
I'll have your Lodgings farther off, and closer,
I'll have no street-lights to you; will you go Sir?

CLAUDIO
I thank ye Sir: the devil take this fortune;
And once more all my service to your goodness.

[Exit.

PENURIO
Now could I eat my very arms for madness,
Cross'd in the nick o' th' matter! vengeance take it,
And that old Cavalier that spoil'd our Cock-fight;
I'll lay the next plot surer.

ISABELLA

I am glad and sorry;
Glad, that I got so fairly off suspition;
Sorry, I lost my new lov'd friend.

PENURIO
Not lost Mistriss;
I'll conjure once again to raise that spirit;
In, and look soberly upon the matter,
We'll ring him one peal more, and if that fall,
The devil tak the Clappers, Bells, and all.

[Exeunt.

ACTUS TERTIUS

SCÆNA PRIMA

Enter **DUCHESS**, **LORDS**, and **RODOPE**.

DUCHESS
Now Rodope, How do you find my daughter?

RODOPE
Madam, I find her now what you would have her,
What the State wishes her; I urg'd her fault to her,
Open'd her eyes, and made her see the mischief
She was running with a headlong will into,
Made her start at her folly, shake and tremble,
At the meer memory of such an ignorance,
She now contemns his love, hates his remembrance,
Cannot endure to hear the name of Silvio;
His person spits at.

DUCHESS
I am glad to hear this.

RODOPE
And humbly now to your Will, your care, Madam,
Bends her affections, bows her best obedience;
Syenna's Duke, with new eyes now she looks on,
And with a Princely love, fit for his person.
Returns that happiness and joy he look'd for;
The general good of both the neighbor Dukedoms,
Not any private end, or rash affection
She aims at now: hearing the Duke arriv'd too,
(To whom she owes all honor, and all service,)

She charg'd me kneel thus at your Graces feet,
And not to rise without a general pardon.

DUCHESS
She has it, and my love again, my old love,
And with more tenderness I meet this penitence,
Than if she ne'er had started from her honor;
I thank ye Rodope, am bound to thank ye,
And daily to remember this great service,
This honest faithful service; go in peace,
And by this Ring, delivered to Bartello,
Let her enjoy our favour, and her liberty,
And presently to this place, with all honor,
See her conducted.

RODOPE
Your Grace has made me happy.

[Exit.

[Enter **1ST LORD**.

1ST LORD
Syenna's noble Duke, craves his admittance.

[Enter **DUKE of SYENNA** with **ATTENDANTS**.

DUCHESS
Go; wait upon his Grace; fair Sir, you are welcome,
Welcome to her ever admir'd your virtues:
And now methinks, my Court looks truly noble;
You have taken too much pains Sir.

DUKE of SYENNA
Royal Lady,
To wait upon your Grace is but my service.

DUCHESS
Keep that Sir, for the Saint ye have vow'd it to.

DUKE of SYENNA
I keep a life for her: since your Grace pleases
To jump so happily into the matter,
I come indeed to claim your Royal promise,
The beauteous Belvidere in marriage,
I come to tender her my youth, my fortune,
My everlasting love.

[Enter **BELVIDERE, BARTELLO, RODOPE, ATTENDANTS.**

DUCHESS
You are like to win, Sir:
All is forgot, forgiven too; no sadness
My good Child, you have the same heart still here,
The Duke of Syenna, Child, pray use him nobly.

DUKE of SYENNA
An Angel beauty.

BELVIDERE
Your Grace is fairly welcome,
And what in modesty a blushing maid may
Wish to a Gentleman of your great goodness;
But wishes are too poor a pay for Princes.

DUKE of SYENNA
You have made me richer than all States and Titles,
One kiss of this white hand's above all honors,
My faith dear Lady, and my fruitful service,
My duteous zeal—

BELVIDERE
Your Grace is a great Master,
And speaks too powerfully to be resisted:
Once more you are welcome, Sir, to me you are welcome,
To her that honors ye; I could say more Sir,
But in anothers tongue 'twere better spoken.

DUKE of SYENNA
As wise as fair, you have made your servant happy;
I never saw so rich a Mine of sweetness.

DUCHESS
Will your Grace please, after your painful journey
To take some rest? Are the Dukes Lodgings ready?

LORD
All Madam.

DUCHESS
Then wait upon his Grace, all, and to morrow, Sir,
We'll shew ye in what high esteem we hold ye,
Till then a fair repose.

DUKE of SYENNA
My fairest service.

[Exit **DUKE of SYENNA** &c.

DUCHESS
You have so honour'd me, my dearest daughter,
So truly pleas'd me in this entertainment,
I mean your loving carriage to Syenna,
That both for ever I forget all trespasses,
And to secure you next of my full favour,
Ask what you will within my power to grant ye,
Ask freely: and if I forget my promise—
Ask confidently.

BELVIDERE
You are too Royal to me;
To me that have so foolishly transgress'd you,
So like a Girl, so far forgot my virtue,
Which now appears as base and ugly to me,
As did his Dream, that thought he was in Paradise,
Awak'd and saw the Devil; how was I wander'd?
With what eies could I look upon that poor, that cours thing,
That wretched thing call'd Sylvio? that (now) despis'd thing,
And lose an object of that graceful sweetness,
That god-like presence as Syenna is?
Darkness, and cheerful day, had not such difference:
But I must ever bless your care, your wisdom,
That led me from this labyrinth of folly,
How had I sunk else? what example given?

DUCHESS
Prethee no more, and as thou art my best one,
Ask something that may equal such a goodness.

BELVIDERE
Why did ye let him go so slightly from ye,
More like a man in triumph, than condemn'd:
Why did ye make his pennance but a question,
A Riddle, every idle wit unlocks.

DUCHESS
'Tis not so,
Nor do not fear it so: he will not find it,
I have given that (unless my self discover it)
Will cost his head.

BELVIDERE
'Tis subject to construction?

DUCHESS
That it is too.

BELVIDERE
It may be then absolv'd,
And then are we both scorn'd and laugh'd at, Madam;
Beside the promise you have ty'd upon it,
Which you must never keep.

DUCHESS
I never meant it.

BELVIDERE
For heaven sake let me know it, 'tis my Suit to ye,
The Boon you would have me ask; let me but see it,
That if there be a way to make't so strong,
No wit nor powerful reason can run through it,
For my disgrace, I may beg of heaven to grant it.

DUCHESS
Fear not, it has been put to sharper judgements
Than e'er he shall arrive at: my dear Father,
That was as fiery in his understanding,
And ready in his wit as any living,
Had it two years, and studied it, yet lost it:
This night ye are my Bed-fellow, there Daughter
Into your bosom I'll commit this secret,
And there we'll both take counsel.

BELVIDERE
I shall find
Some trick I hope too strong yet for his mind.

[Exeunt.

SCÆNA SECUNDA

Enter **PENURIO**.

PENURIO
Methinks I am batten'd well of late, grown lusty,
Fat, high, and kicking, thanks to the bounteous Rugio;
And now, methinks I scorn these poor repasts,
Cheese-parings, and the stinking tongues of Pilchers;
But why should I remember these? they are odious,
They are odious in mine eyes; the full fat dish now,

The bearing dish is that I reverence,
The dish an able Serving-man sweats under,
And bends i' th' hams, as if the house hung on him,
That dish is the dish: hang your bladder Bankets,
Or halfe a dozen of Turnops and two Mushrumps,
These when they breed their best, hatch but two belches;
The state of a fat Turkey, the decorum
He marches in with, all the train and circumstance;
'Tis such a matter, such a glorious matter,
And then his sauce with Oranges and Onions,
And he displaid in all parts, for such a dish now,
And at my need I would betray my Father,
And for a rosted Conger, all my Countrey.

[Enter **BARTELLO**.

BARTELLO
What my friend Lean-gut, how does thy beauteous Mistriss?
And where's your Master Sirrah? where's that horn-pipe?

PENURIO
My Mistriss, Sir, does as a poor wrong'd Gentlewoman,
Too much, heaven knows, opprest with injuries;
May do and live.

BARTELLO
Is the old fool still jealous?

PENURIO
As old fools are, and will be still the same, Sir.

BARTELLO
He must have cause: he must have cause.

PENURIO
'Tis true, Sir,
And would he had with all my heart.

BARTELLO
He shall have.

PENURIO
For then he had Salt to his Saffron porridge.

BARTELLO
Why do not I see thee sometime? why thou starv'd rascal?
Why do not ye come to me, you precious bow-case?
I keep good meat at home, good store.

PENURIO
Yes Sir, I will not fail ye all next week.

BARTELLO
Thou art welcome,
I have a secret I would fain impart to thee,
But thou art so thin, the wind will blow it from thee,
Or men will read it through thee.

PENURIO
Wrap't up in beef Sir,
In good gross beef, let all the world look on me,
The English have that trick to keep intelligence.

BARTELLO
A witty knave, first there's to tie your tongue up.

PENURIO
Dumb as a Dog, Sir.

BARTELLO
Next, hark in your ear, Sirrah.

PENURIO
Well, very well, excellent well: 'tis done, Sir,
Say no more to me.

BARTELLO
Say and hold.

PENURIO
'Tis done, Sir.

BARTELLO
As thou lov'st butter'd eggs, swear.

PENURIO
Let me kiss the Book first,
But here's my hand, brave Captain.

BARTELLO
Look ye hold, sirrah.

[Exit.

PENURIO
Oh the most precious vanity of this world;

When such dry'd Neats-tongues must be soak'd and larded
With young fat supple wenches! Oh the Devil.
What can he do, he cannot suck an egg off
But his back's loose i'th' hilts: go thy wayes Captain,
Well may thy warlike name work Miracles,
But if e'er thy founder'd courser win match more,
Or stand right but one train—

[Enter three **GENTLEMEN**.

1ST GENTLEMAN
Now Signior Shadow,
What art thou thinking of, how to rob thy Master?

PENURIO
Of his good deeds? The Thief that undertakes that
Must have a hook will poze all Hell to hammer:
Have ye dined Gentlemen, or do you purpose?

2ND GENTLEMAN
Dined, two long hours ago.

PENURIO
Pray ye take me with ye.

3RD GENTLEMAN
To supper dost thou mean?

PENURIO
To any thing
That has the smell of meat in't: tell me true, Gentlemen,
Are not you three going to be sinful?
To iropard a joynt, or so? I have found your faces,
And see whore written in your eyes.

1ST GENTLEMAN
A parlous rascal,
Thou art much upon the matter.

PENURIO
Have a care Gentlemen,
'Tis a sore age, very sore age, lewd age,
And women now are like old Knights adventures,
Full of inchanted flames, and dangerous.

2ND GENTLEMAN
Where the most danger is, there's the most honor.

PENURIO
I grant ye, honor most consists in sufferance,
And by that rule you three should be most honorable.

3RD GENTLEMAN
A subtle Rogue: but canst thou tell Penurio
Where we may light upon—

PENURIO
A learned Surgeon?

3RD GENTLEMAN
Pox take ye fool; I mean good wholsome wenches.

PENURIO
'Faith wholsome women will but spoil ye too,
For you are so us'd to snap-haunces: But take my counsel,
Take fat old women, fat, and five and fifty,
The Dog-dayes are come in.

2ND GENTLEMAN
Take fat old women?

PENURIO
The fatter and the older, still the better,
You do not know the pleasure of an old Dame,
A fat old Dame, you do not know the knack on't:
They are like our countrey Grotts, as cool as Christmas,
And sure i' th' keels.

1ST GENTLEMAN
Hang him starv'd fool: he mocks us.

3RD GENTLEMAN
Penurio, thou know'st all the handsome wenches?
What shall I give thee for a Merchants wife now?

PENURIO
I take no money Gentlemen, that's base,
I trade in meat, a Merchants wife will cost ye
A glorious Capon; a great shoulder of Mutton;
And a Tart as big as a Conjurers Circle.

3RD GENTLEMAN
That's cheap enough.

1ST GENTLEMAN
And what a Haberdashers?

PENURIO

Worse meat will serve for her, a great Goose-Pie,
But you must send it out o' th' Countrey to me,
It will not do else: with a piece of Bacon,
And if you can, a pot of Butter with it.

2ND GENTLEMAN

Now do I aim at horse-flesh: what a Parsons?

PENURIO

A Tithe-Pig has no fellow, if I fetch her,
If she be Puritane, Plumb-porridge does it,
And a fat loin of Veal, well sauc'd and roasted.

2ND GENTLEMAN

We'll meet one night, and thou shalt have all these;
O' that condition we may have the wenches
A dainty rascal.

PENURIO

When your stomachs serve ye,
(For mine is ever ready) I'll supply ye.

1ST GENTLEMAN

Farewel, and there's to fill thy paunch.

PENURIO

Brave Gentleman.

2ND GENTLEMAN

Hold sirrah, there.

PENURIO

Any young wench i' th' Town, Sir.

3RD GENTLEMAN

It shall go round.

[Exit **GENTLEMEN**.

PENURIO

Most honorable Gentlemen,
All these are Courtiers, but they are meer Coxcombs,
And only for a wench, their purses open,
Nor have they so much judgement left to chuse her;
If e'r they call upon me, I'll so fit 'em,
I have a pack of wry-mouth'd mackrel Ladies,

Stink like a standing ditch, and those dear Damsels;
But I forget my business, I thank ye Monsieurs,
I have a thousand whimseys in my brain now.

[Exit.

Enter to a Banquet **DUCHESS, DUKE of SYENNA, LORDS, ATTENDANTS.**

DUCHESS
Your Grace shall now perceive how much we honor ye
And in what dear regard we hold your friendship:
Will you sit Sir, and grace this homely Banquet?

DUKE of SYENNA
Madam, to your poor friend, you are too magnificent.

DUCHESS
To the Dukes health, and all the joyes I wish him,
Let no man miss this cup: have we no Musick?

DUKE of SYENNA
Your noble favours still you heap upon me,
But where's my virtuous Mistriss, such a Feast,
And not her sparkling beauty here to bless it?
Methinks it should not be, it shews not fully.

DUCHESS
Young Ladies Sir; are long, and curious
In putting on their trims, forget how day goes,
And then 'tis their good morrow when they are ready:
Go some and call her, and wait upon her hither,
Tell her the Duke and I desire her company:
I warrant ye, a hundred dressings now
She has survey'd, this, and that fashion look'd on,
For Ruffs and Gowns; cast this away, these Jewels
Suited to these and these knots: o' my life Sir,
She fears your curious eye will soon discover else:
Why stand ye still, why gape ye on one another?
Did I not bid ye go, and tell my Daughter?
Are ye nailed here? nor stir? nor speak? who am I,
And who are you?

1ST LORD
Pardon me, gracious Lady,

The fear to tell you that you would not hear of
Makes us all dumb, the Princess is gone, Madam.

DUCHESS
Gone? whither gone? some wiser fellow answer me.

2ND LORD
We sought the Court all over, and believe Lady
No news of where she is, nor how convey'd hence.

DUCHESS
It cannot be, it must not be.

1ST LORD
'Tis true, Madam,
No room in all the Court, but we search'd through it,
Her women found her want first, and they cry'd to us.

DUCHESS
Gone? stol'n away? I am abus'd, dishonour'd.

DUKE of SYENNA
'Tis I that am abus'd, 'tis I dishonour'd.
Is this your welcome, this your favour to me?
To foist a trick upon me, this trick too,
To cheat me of my love? Am I not worthy?
Or since I was your guest, am I grown odious?

DUCHESS
Your Grace mistakes me, as I have a life, Sir.

DUKE of SYENNA
And I another, I will never bear this,
Never endure this dor.

DUCHESS
But hear me patiently.

DUKE of SYENNA
Give me my Love.

DUCHESS
As soon as care can find her,
And all care shall be used.

DUKE of SYENNA
And all my care too,
To be reveng'd; I smell the trick, 'tis too rank,

Fie, how it smells o' th' Mother.

DUCHESS
You wrong me, Duke.

DUKE of SYENNA
For this disgrace ten thousand Florentines
Shall pay their dearest bloods, and dying curse ye,
And so I turn away, your mortal enemy.

[Exit.

DUCHESS
Since ye are so high and hot Sir, ye have half arm'd us,
Be careful of the Town, of all the Castles,
And see supplies of Soldiers every where,
And Musters for the Field when he invites us,
For he shall know 'tis not high words can fright us.
My Daughter gone? has she so finely cozen'd me?
This is for Silvio's sake sure, Oh cunning false one;
Publish a Proclamation thorough the Dukedom.
That whosoe'er can bring to th' Court young Silvio,
Alive or dead, beside our thanks and favour,
Shall have two thousand Duckets for his labour;
See it dispatch'd, and sent in haste: Oh base one.

[Exeunt.

SCÆNA QUARTA

Enter **ISABELLA** and **PENURIO** with a Light.

ISABELLA
Was't thou with Rugio?

PENURIO
Yes marry was I closely.

ISABELLA
And does he still remember his poor Mistriss?
Does he desire to see me?

PENURIO
Yes, and presently:
Puts off all business else, lives in that memory,
And will be here according to directions.

ISABELLA
But where's thy Master?

PENURIO
Where a coxcomb should be,
Waiting at Court with his Jewels,
Safe for this night I warrant ye.

ISABELLA
I am bound to thee.

PENURIO
I would ye were, as close as I could tye ye.

ISABELLA
Thou art my best, my truest friend.

PENURIO
I labour
I moil and toil for ye: I am your hackney.

ISABELLA
If ever I be able—

PENURIO
Steal the great Cheese Mistriss,
Was sent him out o'th' Countrey.

ISABELLA
Any thing.

PENURIO
That's meat, 'tis lawful Mistriss: where's the Castle Custard
He got at Court?

ISABELLA
He has lock'd it in's study.

PENURIO
Get a warrant to search for counterfeit Gold.

ISABELLA
Give me thy Candle,
I'll find a time to be thy careful Cater.

PENURIO
And many a time I'll find to be his Cook,

And dress his Calves head to the sweetest sauce Mistriss.

ISABELLA
To bed Penurio, go, the rest is my charge,
I'll keep the Watch out.

PENURIO
Now if you spare him—

[Exit.

ISABELLA
Peace fool,
I hope my Rugio will not fail, 'twould vex me:
Now to my string; so, sure he cannot miss now,
And this end to my finger: I'll lie down,
For on a suddain I am wondrous heavy,
'Tis very late too; if he come and find this,
And pull it, though it be with easie motion
I shall soon waken, and as soon be with him.

[Enter **LOPEZ**.

LOPEZ
Thou secret friend, how am I bound to love thee!
And how to hug thee for thy private service!
Thou art the Star all my suspitions sail by,
The fixed point my wronged honor turns to,
By thee I shall know all, find all the subtilties
Of devilish women, that torment me daily:
Thou art my Conjurer, my Spell, my Spirit,
All's hush'd and still, no sound of any stirring,
No tread of living thing: the Light is in still,
And there's my Wife, how prettily the fool lies,
How sweet, and handsomely, and in her clothes too,
Waiting for me upon my life; her fondness
Would not admit her rest till I came to her:
O careful fool, why am I angry with thee?
Why do I think thou hat'st thy loving Husband?
I am an Ass, an over-doting Coxcomb,
And this sweet soul, the mirror of perfection:
How admirable fair and delicate,
And how it stirs me, I'll sing thy sweets a Requiem,
But will not waken thee.

SONG.
Oh fair sweet face, oh eyes celestial bright,
Twin Stars in Heaven, that now adorn the night;

Oh fruitful Lips, where Cherries ever grow,
And Damask cheeks, where all sweet beauties blow;
Oh thou from head to foot divinely fair,
Cupid's most cunning Nets made of that hair,
And as he weaves himself for curious eyes;
Oh me, Oh me, I am caught my self, he cries:
Sweet rest about thee sweet and golden sleep,
Soft peaceful thoughts, your hourly watches keep,
Whilst I in wonder sing this sacrifice,
To beauty sacred, and those Angel-eyes.

Now will I steal a kiss, a dear kiss from her,
And suck the Rosie breath of this bright beauty;
What a Devil is this? ty'd to her finger too?
A string, a damned string to give intelligence
Oh my lov'd key, how truly hast thou serv'd me;
I'll follow this: soft, soft, to th' door it goes,
And through to th' other side; a damned string 'tis,
I am abus'd, topt, cuckolded, fool'd, jaded,
Ridden to death, to madness; stay, this helps not:
Stay, stay, and now invention help me,
I'll sit down by her, take this from her easily,
And thus upon mine own: Dog, I shall catch ye,
With all your cunning, Sir: I shall light on ye,
I felt it pull sure: yes, but wondrous softly,
'Tis there again, and harder now, have at ye,
Now and thou scap'st, the Devil's thy ghostly father.

[Exit.

ISABELLA
Sure 'twas my husband's voice, the string is gone too,
He has found the trick on't: I am undone, betray'd,
And if he meet my friend he perishes,
What fortune follows me, what spightful fortune?
Hoa Jaquenet.

[Enter **JAQUENET**.

JAQUENET
Here Mistriss, do you call me?

ISABELLA
Didst thou hear no noise?

JAQUENET
I hear my Master mad yonder,
And swears, and chafes—

ISABELLA
Dar'st thou do one thing for me?
One thing concerns mine honor, all is lost else?

JAQUENET
Name what you will.

ISABELLA
It can bring but a beating,
Which I will recompence so largely—

JAQUENET
Name it.

ISABELLA
Sit here, as if thou wert asleep.

JAQUENET
Is that all?

ISABELLA
When he comes in, whate'er he do unto thee
(The worst will be but beating) speak not a word,
Not one word as thou lovest me.

JAQUENET
I'll run through it.

ISABELLA
I'll carry away the Candle.

[Exit.

JAQUENET
And I the blows Mistriss.

[Enter **LOPEZ**.

LOPEZ
Have you put your light out? I shall stumble to ye,
You whore, you cunning whore, I shall catch your rogue too,
H'as light legs else, I had so Ferret-claw'd him:
Oh have I found ye? do ye play at dog-sleep still whore?
Do you think that can protect ye? yes, I will kill thee,
But first I'll bring thy friends to view thy villanies,
Thy whorish villanies: and first I'll beat thee,
Beat thee to pin-dust, thou salt whore, thou varlet,

Scratch out thine eyes; I'll spoil your tempting visage;
Are ye so patient? I'll put my nails in deeper,
Is it good whoring? whoring ye base rascal?
Is it good tempting men with strings to ride ye?
So, I'll fetch your kindred, and your friends, whore,
And such a Justice I will act upon thee.

[Exit.

[Enter **ISABELLA**.

ISABELLA
What is he gone?

JAQUENET
The Devil go with him Mistriss,
Has harrowed me, plough'd Land was ne'r so harrow'd:
I had the most adoe to save mine eyes.

ISABELLA
Has paid thee,
But I'll heal all again with good Gold. Jaquenet;
H'as damned nails.

JAQUENET
They are ten-penny nails I think Mistriss:
I'll undertake he shall strike 'em through an inch board.

ISABELLA
Go up, and wash thy self: take my Pomatum,
And now let me alone to end the Tragedy.

JAQUENET
You had best beware.

ISABELLA
I shall deal stoutly with him,
Reach me my Book, and see the door made fast wench,
And so good night: now to the matter politick.

[**LOPEZ** knocks within.

LOPEZ
Within. You shall see what she is, what a sweet jewel.

ISABELLA
Who's there, what mad-man knocks? is this an hour
And in mine Husband's absence?

LOPEZ
Within. Will ye open?
You know my voice ye whore, I am that Husband:
Do you mark her subtilty? but I have paid her,
I have so ferk'd her face: here's the blood Gentlemen,
Ecce signum: I have spoil'd her Goatish beauty,
Observe her how she looks now, how she is painted,
Oh 'tis the most wicked'st whore, and the most treacherous—

[Enter **LOPEZ**, **BARTELLO**, **GENTLEMAN** and two **GENTLEWOMEN**.

GENTLEMAN
Here walks my cosin full of meditation,
Arm'd with religious thoughts.

BARTELLO
Is this the monster?

1ST GENTLEWOMAN
Is this the subject of that rage you talk'd of,
That naughty woman you had pull'd a-pieces?

BARTELLO
Here's no such thing.

1ST GENTLEWOMAN
How have ye wrong'd this beauty?
Are not you mad my friend? what time o' th' moon is 't?
Have not you Maggots in your brains?

LOPEZ
'Tis she sure.

GENTLEMAN
Where's the scratch'd face ye spoke of, the torn garments,
And all the hair pluck'd off her head?

BARTELLO
Believe me,
'Twere better far you had lost your pair of pibbles,
Than she the least adornment of that sweetness.

LOPEZ
Is not this blood?

1ST GENTLEWOMAN
This is a monstrous folly,

A base abuse.

ISABELLA
Thus he does ever use me,
And sticks me up a wonder, not a woman,
Nothing I doe, but's subject to suspition;
Nothing I can do, able to content him.

BARTELLO
Lopez, you must not use this.

2ND GENTLEWOMAN
'Twere not amiss, Sir,
To give ye sauce to your meat, and suddainly.

1ST GENTLEWOMAN
You that dare wrong a woman of her goodness,
Thou have a Wife, thou have a Bear ty'd to thee,
To scratch thy jealous itch, were all o' my mind,
I mean all women, we would soone disburthen ye
Of that that breeds these fits, these dog-flaws in ye,
A Sow-guelder should trim ye.

BARTELLO
A rare cure Lady,
And one as fit for him as a Thief for a halter,
You see this youth: will you not cry him quittance,
Body 'me, I would pine, but I would pepper him,
I'll come anon, he, hang him, poor pompillion:
How like a wench bepist he looks, I'll come Lady;
Lopez, The Law must teach ye what a wife is,
A good, a virtuous wife.

ISABELLA
I'll ne'r live with him,
I crave your loves all to make known my cause,
That so a fair Divorce may pass between us,
I am weary of my life: in danger hourly.

BARTELLO
You see how rude you are, I will not miss ye,
Unsufferable rude: I'll pay him soundly,
You should be whipt in Bedlam: I'll reward him.

2ND GENTLEWOMAN
Whipping's too good.

LOPEZ

I think I am alive still,
And in my wits.

BARTELLO
I'll put a trick upon him,
And get his goods confiscate: you shall have 'em;
I will not fail at nine.

LOPEZ
I think I am here too,
And once I would have sworn I had taken her napping,
I think my name is Lopez.

GENTLEMAN
Fie for shame, Sir,
You see you have abus'd her, fouly wrong'd her,
Hung scandalous and course opinions on her,
Which now you find but children of suspition:
Ask her forgiveness, shew a penitence,
She is my kinswoman, and what she suffers
Under so base and beastly jealousies,
I will redress else, I'll seek satisfaction.

BARTELLO
Why, every boy i' th' Town will piss upon thee.

LOPEZ
I am sorry for't.

1ST GENTLEWOMAN
Down o' your marrow-bones.

LOPEZ
Even sorry from my heart: forgive me sweet wife,
Here I confess most freely I have wrong'd ye,
As freely here I beg a pardon of ye,
From this hour no debate, no cross suspition—

ISABELLA
To shew ye Sir I understand a wives part,
Thus I assure my love, and seal your pardon.

2ND GENTLEWOMAN
'Tis well done, now to bed, and there confirm it.

GENTLEMAN
And so good night.

BARTELLO
Aware relapses, Lopez.

[Exeunt.

LOPEZ
Now Isabella tell me truth, and suddainly,
And do not juggle with me, nor dissemble,
For as I have a life ye dye then: I am not mad,
Nor does the Devil work upon my weakness,
Tell me the trick of this, and tell me freely.

ISABELLA
Will then that satisfie ye?

LOPEZ
If ye deal ingeniously.

ISABELLA
I'll tell ye all; and tell ye true and freely.
Bartello was the end of all this jealousie,
His often visitations brought by you, first
Bred all these fits, and these suspitions:
I knew your false key, and accordingly
I fram'd my plot, to have you take him finely,
Too poor a pennance for the wrong his wife bears,
His worthy virtuous wife: I felt it sensibly
When ye took off the string, and was much pleas'd in't,
Because I wish'd his importunate dotage paid well,
And had you staid two minutes more, ye had had him.

LOPEZ
This sounds like truth.

ISABELLA
Because this shall be certain,
Next time he comes, as long he cannot tarry,
Your self shall see, and hear, his lewd temptations.

LOPEZ
Till then I am satisfied, and if this prove true,
Hence-forward Mistriss of your self I give ye,
And I to serve ye: For my lusty Captain,
I'll make him dance, and make him think the Devil
Claws at his breech, and yet I will not hurt him:
Come now to bed, and prove but constant this way,
I'll prove the man you ever wished.

ISABELLA
You have blest me.

[Exeunt.

Enter **SILVIO**.

SILVIO
What labour and what travel have I run through
And through what Cities to absolve this Riddle
Diviners, Dreamers, School-men, deep Magicians,
All have I try'd, and all give several meaning,
And from all hope of any future happiness,
To this place am I come at length, the Countrey,
The people simple, plain, and harmless witty,
Whose honest labours Heaven rewards with plenty
Of Corn, Wine, Oyl, which they again as thankful,
To their new Crops, new pastimes celebrate,
And crown their joyful harvests with new voices;
By a rich Farmer here I am entertain'd,
And rank'd among the number of his servants,
Not guessing what I am, but what he would have me,
Here may be so much wit (though much I fear it)
To undo this knotty question; and would to Heaven.

[Enter **SOTO** with a Proclamation.

My fortunes had been hatch'd with theirs, as innocent,
And never known a pitch above their plainness.

SOTO
That it is, that it is, what's this word now? this
Is a plaguy word, that it is r. e. a. that it is, reason,
By your leave, Mr. Soto, by your leave, you are too quick, Sir,
There's a strange parlous T. before the reason,
A very tall T. which makes the word High Treason.

SILVIO
What Treason's that? does this fellow understand
Himself?

SOTO

Pitch will infect, I'll meddle no more with this geer;
What a devil ails this fellow? this foolish fellow?
Being admitted to be one of us too,
That are the masters of the sports proceeding,
Thus to appear before me too, unmorris'd?
Do you know me friend?

SILVIO

You are my Masters Son, Sir.

SOTO

And do you know what sports are now in season?

SILVIO

I hear there are some a-foot.

SOTO

Where are your Bells then?
Your Rings, your Ribons, friend? & your clean Napkins?
Your Nosegay in your hat, pinn'd up, am not I here?
My fathers eldest Son, and at this time, Sir,
I would have ye know it, though ye be ten times his servant
A better man than my father far, Lord of this Harvest, Sir,
And shall a man of my place want attendance?

SILVIO

'Twas want of knowledge, Sir, not duty, bred this,
I would have made Suit else for your Lordships service.

SOTO

In some sort I am satisfied now, mend your manners,
But thou art a melancholy fellow, vengeance melancholy,
And that may breed an insurrection amongst us;
Go too, I'll lay the best part of two pots now
Thou art in love, and I can guess with whom too,
I saw the wench that twir'd and twinkled at thee,
The other day; the wench that's new come hither,
The young smug wench.

SILVIO

You know more than I feel Sir.

SOTO

Go too, I'll be thy friend, I'll speak a good word for thee,
And thou shalt have my Lordships countenance to her;
May be I have had a snap my self, may be I, may be no,
We Lords are allow'd a little more.

SILVIO
'Tis fit, Sir;
I humbly thank ye, you are too too tender of me,
But what Sir, I beseech ye, was that paper,
Your Lordship was so studiously imployed in,
When ye came out a-doors?

SOTO
Thou meanest this paper.

SILVIO
That Sir, I think.

SOTO
Why, 'tis a Proclamation,
A notable piece of villany, as ever thou heard'st in thy life,
By mine honor it is.

SILVIO
How Sir? or what concerns it?

SOTO
It comes ye from the Dutchess, a plaguy wise woman,
To apprehend the body of one Silvio,
As arrant a Rascal as ever pist against a post,
And this same Silvio, or this foresaid rascal,
To bring before her, live or dead; for which good service
The man that brings him, has two thousand Duckets;
Is not this notable matter now?

SILVIO
'Tis so indeed,
This Proclamation bears my bane about it;
Can no rest find me? no private place secure me?
But still my miseries like blood-hounds haunt me?
Unfortunate young man, which way now guides thee,
Guides thee from death? the Countrey's laid round for thee;
Oh Claudio, now I feel thy blood upon me,
Now it speaks loudly here, I am sure against me,
Time now has found it out, and truth proclaim'd it,
And Justice now cries out, I must die for it.

SOTO
Hast thou read it?

SILVIO
Yes.

SOTO
And dost thou know that Silvio.

SILVIO
I never saw him, Sir.

SOTO
I have, and know him too,
I know him as well as I know thee, and better,
And if I light upon him, for a trick he plaid me once,
A certain kind of dog-trick, I'll so fiddle him,
Two thousand Duckets, I'll so pepper him,
And with that money I'll turn Gentleman,
Worth a brown Baker's dozen of such Silvios.

SILVIO
There is no staying here, this rogue will know me,
And for the money sake betray me too;
I must bethink me suddenly and safely.

[Enter **MORRIS-DANCERS**.

SOTO
Mine own dear Lady, have-at-thy honey-comb,
Now, for the honor of our Town, Boyes, trace sweetly.

[Cry within]
Arm, Arm.

What a vengeance ails this whobub: pox refuse 'em,
Cannot they let us dance in our own defence here?

[Enter **FARMER** and **CAPTAIN**.

CAPTAIN
Arm, honest friends, arm suddenly and bravely,
And with your antient resolutions follow me;
Look how the Beacons show like Comets, your poor neighbors
Run maddingly affrighted through the Villages;
Syenna's Duke is up, burns all before him,
And with his sword, makes thousand mothers childless.

SOTO
What's this to our Morris-dancers?

SILVIO
This may serve my turn.

SOTO
There's ne'r a Duke in Christendom but loves a May-game.

CAPTAIN
At a horse you were always ceaz'd, put your Son on him,
And arm him well i' th' States name, I command ye;
And they that dare go voluntary, shall receive reward.

SOTO
I dare go no way, Sir, this is strange, Master Captain,
You cannot be content to spoil our sport here,
Which I do not think your Worship's able to answer,
But you must set us together by the ears with I know not who too?
We are for the bodily part o' th' dance.

CAPTAIN
Arm him suddainly,
This is no time to fool, I shall return ye else,
A rebel to the General, State, and Duchess,
And how you'll answer then—

FARMER
I have no more Sons, Sir,
This is my only boy; I beseech ye Master Captain.

SOTO
I am a rank coward too, to say the truth, Sir,
I never had good luck at buffets neither.

FARMER
Here's vorty shillings, spare the child.

CAPTAIN
I cannot.

SOTO
Are ye a man? will ye cast away a May-Lord?
Shall all the wenches in the Countrey curse ye?

SILVIO
An't please you Captain, I'll supply his person,
'Tis pity their old custom should be frighted,
Let me have Horse, and good Arms, I'll serve willingly,
And if I shrink a foot of ground, Hell take me.

CAPTAIN
A promising Aspect, face full of courage,
I'll take this man, and thank ye too.

FARMER
There's for thee,
'Tis in a clout, but good old Gold.

SILVIO
I thank ye Sir.

FARMER
Goe saddle my fore-horse, put his feather on too,
He'll praunce it bravely, friend, he fears no Colours,
And take the Armor down, and see him dizin'd.

SOTO
Farewel, and if thou cary'st thy self well in this matter,
I say no more, but this, there must be more May-Lords,
And I know who are fit.

SILVIO
Dance you, I'll fight, Sir.

CAPTAIN
Away, away.

SILVIO
Farewel, I am for the Captain.

[Exit.

FARMER
Now to this matter again my honest fellows,
For if this goe not forward, I foresee friends,
This war will fright our neighbors out o' th' villages;
Cheer up your hearts, we shall hear better news, boys.

BOMBY
Surely I will dance no more, 'tis most ridiculous,
I find my wives instructions now mere verities,
My learned wives, she often hath pronounc'd to me
My safety Bomby, defie these sports, thou art damn'd else,
This Beast of Babylon, I will never back again,
His pace is sure prophane, and his lewd Wi-hees,
The Sons of Hymyn and Gymyn, in the wilderness.

FARMER
Fie neighbor Bomby, in your fits again,
Your zeal sweats, this is not careful, neighbor,
The Hobby-horse, is a seemly Hobby-horse.

SOTO
And as pretty a beast on's inches, though I say it.

BOMBY
The Beast is an unseemly, and a lewd Beast,
And got at Rome by the Popes Coach-Horses,
His mother was the Mare of ignorance.

SOTO
Cobler thou ly'st, and thou wert a thousand Coblers.
His mother was an honest Mare, and a Mare of good credit,
I know the Mare, and if need be, can bring witness;
And in the way of honesty I tell thee,
Scorn'd any Coach-Horse the Pope had: thou art foolish,
And thy blind zeal makes thee abuse the Beast.

BOMBY
I do defie thee, and thy foot-cloth too,
And tell thee to thy face, this prophane riding
I feel it in my conscience, and I dare speak it,
This un-edified ambling, hath brought a scourge upon us,
This Hobby-horse sincerity we liv'd in
War, and the sword of slaughter: I renounce it,
And put the beast off; thus, the beast polluted,
And now no more shall hop on high Bomby,
Follow the painted pipes of high pleasures,
And with the wicked, dance the devils measures;
Away thou pamper'd jade of vanity,
Stand at the Livery of lewd delights now,
And eat the provinder of prick-ear'd folly,
My dance shall be to the pipe of persecution.

FARMER
Will you daunce no more neighbor?

BOMBY
Surely no,
Carry the Beast to his Crib: I have renounc'd him
And all his works.

SOTO
Shall the Hobby-horse be forgot then?
The hopeful Hobby-horse, shall he lye founder'd?
If thou do'st this, thou art but a cast-away Cobler:
My anger's up, think wisely, and think quickly,
And look upon the quondam beast of pleasure,
If thou dost this (mark me, thou serious Sowter)

Thou Bench-whistler of the old tribe of toe-pieces,
If thou dost this, there shall be no more shooe-mending,
Every man shall have a special care of his own soul:
And in his pocket carry his two Confessors,
His Yugel, and his Nawl: if thou dost this—

FARMER
He will dance again for certain.

BOMBY
I cry out on't,
'Twas the fore-running sin brought in those Tilt-staves,
They brandish 'gainst the Church, the devil calls May-poles.

SOTO
Take up your Horse again, and girth him to ye,
And girth him handsomely, good neighbor Bomby.

BOMBY
I spit at him.

SOTO
Spit in the Horse face, Cobler?
Thou out of tune, Psalm-singing slave; spit in his visnomy?

BOMBY
I spit again, and thus I rise against him:
Against this Beast: that signify'd destruction.
Fore-shew'd i'th' falls of Monarchies.

SOTO
I'th' face of him?
Spit such another spit by this hand Cobler
I'll make ye set a new piece o' your nose there,
Tak't up I say, and dance without more bidding,
And dance as you were wont: you have been excellent
And art still, but for this new nicity,
And your wives learned Lectures: take up the Hobby-horse
Come, 'tis a thing thou hast lov'd with all thy heart Bomby,
And would'st do still but for the round-breech'd brothers:
You were not thus in the morning: tak't up I say,
Do not delay but do it: you know I am officer;
And I know 'tis unfit all these good fellows
Should wait the cooling of your zealous porridge;
Chuse whether you will dance, or have me execute:
I'll clap your neck i' th' stocks, and there I'll make ye
Dance a whole day, and dance with these at night too,
You mend old shooes well, mend your old manners better,

And suddenly see you leave off this sincereness.
This new hot Batch, borrowed from some brown Baker,
Some learned brother, or I'll so bait ye for't,
Take it quickly up.

BOMBY
I take my persecution,
And thus I am forc'd a by-word to my brethren.

SOTO
Strike up, strike up: strike merrily.

FARMER
To it roundly,
Now to the harvest feast: then sport again boyes.

[Exeunt.

SCÆNA SECUNDA

Enter **SILVIO**, arm'd.

SILVIO
What shall I do? live thus unknown, and base still?
Or thrust my self into the head o' th' Battel?
And there like that I am, a Gentleman,
And one that never fear'd the face of danger,
(So in her angry eyes she carried honor)
Fight nobly, and (to end my cares) die nobly?

Song [within]
Silvio go on, and raise thy noble mind
To noble ends; fling course base thoughts behind:
Silvio, thou Son of everliving fame,
Now aim at virtue, and a Noble Name.
Silvio consider, Honor is not won,
Nor virtue reach'd, till some brave thing be done:
Thy Countrey calls thee now; she burns, and bleeds,
Now raise thy self, young man, to noble deeds.
Into the battel Silvio, there seek forth
Danger, and blood, by them stands sacred worth.

What heavenly voice is this that follows me?
This is the second time 't has waited on me,
Since I was arm'd, and ready for the battel;
It names me often, steels my heart with courage.

[Enter **BELVIDERE** deformed.

And in a thousand sweet notes comforts me;
What Beldam's this? how old she is, and ugly,
Why does she follow me?

BELVIDERE
Be not dismaid Son,
I wait upon thee for thy good, and honor,
'Twas I that now sung to thee, stirr'd thy mind up,
And rais'd thy spirits to the pitch of nobleness.

SILVIO
Though she be old, and of a crooked carkass,
Her voice is like the harmony of Angels.

BELVIDERE
Thou art my darling, all my love dwels on thee
The Son of virtue, therefore I attend thee;
Enquire not what I am, I come to serve thee,
For if thou be'st inquisitive, thou hast lost me:
A thousand long miles hence my dwelling is,
Deep in a Cave, where but mine own, no foot treads,
There by mine Art, I found what danger (Silvio)
And deep distress of heart, thou wert grown into,
A thousand Leagues I have cut through empty air,
Far swifter than the sayling rack that gallops
Upon the wings of angry winds, to seek thee.
Sometimes o'er a swelling tide, on a Dolphins back I ride,
Sometimes pass the earth below, and through the unmoved Center go;
Sometimes in a flame of fire, like a Meteor I aspire,
Sometimes in mine own shape, thus, when I help the virtuous,
Men of honourable minds, command my Art in all his kinds;
Pursue the noble thought of War, from thy Guard I'll not be far,
Get thee worship on thy foe, lasting Fame is gotten so.
Single Syennas Duke alone, hear thy friends, thy Countrey groan,
And with thy manly arm strike sure, then thou hast wrought thine own free cure.

SILVIO
Some Sybel sure, some soul heaven loves, and favours.
And lends her their free powers, to work their wonders?
How she incites my courage!

BELVIDERE
Sylvio,
I knew thee many daies ago,
Foresaw thy love to Belvidere, the Dutchess daughter, and her Heir;

Knew she lov'd thee, and know what past; when you were found i' th' Castle fast
In one anothers arms; forsaw the taking of ye and the Law
And so thy innocence I loved, the deepest of my skill I proved;
Be rul'd by me, for to this hour, I have dwelt about thee with my power.

SILVIO
I will, and in the course of all observe thee,
For thou art sure an Angel good sent to me.

BELVIDERE
Get thee gone then to the fight, longer stay but robs thy right;
When thou grow'st weary I'll be near, then think on beauteous Belvidere,
For every precious thought of her, I'll lend thine honor a new spurre;
When all is done, meet here at night; Go and be happy in the fight.

[Exit.

SILVIO
I certainly believe I shall do nobly,
And that I'll bravely reach at too, or die.

[Exeunt.

SCÆNA TERTIA

Enter **CLAUDIO** and **PENURIO**.

CLAUDIO
Is she so loving still?

PENURIO
She is mad with Love,
As mad as ever unworm'd dog was, Signior,
And does so weep, and curse, for your prevention,
Your crosses in your love; it frets me too,
I am fall'n away to nothing, to a spindle,
Grown a meer man of mat, no soul within me,
Pox o' my Master, Sir, will that content ye?

CLAUDIO
This rogue but cozens me, and she neglects me,
Upon my life there are some other gamesters,
Nearer the wind than I, and that prevents me,
Is there no other holds acquaintance with her?
Prethee be true, be honest, do not mock me,
Thou knowest her heart, no former interest

She has vow'd a favour too? and cannot handsomely
Go off, but by regaining such a friendship?
There are a thousand handsome men, young, wealthy,
That will not stick at any rate, nor danger,
To gain so sweet a prize; nor can I blame her,
If where she finds a comfort, she deal cunningly,
I am a stranger yet.

PENURIO
Ye are all she looks for,
And if there be any other, she neglects all,
And all for you: I would you saw how grievously
And with what hourly lamentations.

CLAUDIO
I know thou flatter'st me; tell me but truth,
Look here, look well, the best meat in the Dukedom,
The rarest, and the choicest of all Diets,
This will I give thee, but to satisfie me;
That is, not to dissemble; this rare Lobster,
This Pheasant of the Sea, this dish for Princes,
And all this thou shalt enjoy, eat all thy self,
Have good Greek Wine, or any thing belongs to it,
A wench, if it desire one.

PENURIO
All this, Signior?

CLAUDIO
All, and a greater far than this.

PENURIO
A greater?

CLAUDIO
If thou deserve by telling truth.

PENURIO
A wench too?

CLAUDIO
Or any thing, but if you play the knave now,
The cozening knave, besides the loss of this,
In which thou hast parted with a paradise,
I ne'er will give thee meat more, not a morsel,
No smell of meat by my means shall come near thee,
Nor name of any thing that's nourishing,
But to thy old part Tantalus again,

Thou shalt return, and there snap at a shadow.

PENURIO
Upon this point, had I intended Treason,
Or any thing might call my life in question,
Follow'd with all the tortures time could think on,
Give me but time to eat this lovely Lobster,
This Alderman o'th' Sea, and give me Wine to him,
I would reveal all, and if that all were too little,
More than I knew; Bartello holds in with her,
The Captain of the Cittadel, but you need not fear him,
His tongue's the stiffest weapon that he carries.
He is old, and out of use; there are some other,
Men, young enough, handsome, and bold enough,
Could they come but to make their game once, but they want Sir,
They want the unde quare, they are laid by then.

[Enter **BARTELLO**.

You only are the man shall knock the nail in—

BARTELLO
How now Penurio?

PENURIO
Your worship's fairly met, Sir.
You shall hear further from me, steal aside, Sir.

CLAUDIO
Remember your Master for those Chains.

PENURIO
They are ready, Sir.

BARTELLO
What young thing's this? by his habit he's a Merchant;
I fear he trades my way too, you dryed dog-fish,
What bait was that?

PENURIO
Who Sir, the thing went hence now?
A notable young whelp.

BARTELLO
To what end sirrah?

PENURIO
Came to buy Chains and Rings, is to be married,

An Asse, a Coxcomb, h'as nothing in's house Sir;
I warrant you think he came to see my Mistriss?

BARTELLO
I doubt it shrewdly.

PENURIO
Away, away 'tis foolish;
He has not the face to look upon a Gentlewoman,
A poor skim'd thing, his Mothers maids are fain, Sir
To teach him how to kiss, and against he is married,
To shew him on which side the stirrop stands.

BARTELLO
That's a fine youth.

PENURIO
Thou wouldst hang thy self, that thou hadst half his power,
Thou empty Potgun.

BARTELLO
Am I come fit Penurio?

PENURIO
As fit as a fiddle,
My Master's now abroad about his business.

BARTELLO
When thou cam'st to me home to day, I half suspected
My wife was jealous, that she whispered to thee.

PENURIO
You deserve well the whilst, there's no such matter,
She talk'd about some toyes my Master must bring to her,
You must not know of.

BARTELLO
I'll take no noat Penurio.

PENURIO
No, nor you shall not, till you have it soundly.
This is the bravest Capitano Pompo.

[Enter **ISABELLA**.

But I shall pump ye anon, Sir.

ISABELLA

Oh my Bartello.

BARTELLO
Ye pretty Rogue; you little Rogue, you sweet Rogue,
Away Penurio, go and walk i'th' Horse-Fair.

ISABELLA
You do not love me?

BARTELLO
Thou liest, thou little rascal;
There sirrah, to your Centry.

PENURIO
How the Colt itches.
I'll help ye to a Curry-comb shall claw ye.

[Exit.

ISABELLA
And how much dost thou love me?

BARTELLO
Let's go in quickly,
I'll tell thee presently, I'll measure it to thee.

ISABELLA
No busses first? sit o' my knee, my brave boy,
My valiant boy; do not look so fiercely on me,
Thou wilt fright me with thy face; come buss again Chick,
Smile in my face you mad thing.

BARTELLO
I am mad indeed wench,
Precious, I am all o' fire.

ISABELLA
I'll warm thee better.

BARTELLO
I'll warm thee too, or I'll blow out my bellows;
Ha, ye sweet rogue, you loving rogue, a boy now,
A Soldier I will get shall prove a fellow.

[Enter **JAQUENET** and **PENURIO**.

JAQUENET
Mistriss, look to your self, my Master's coming.

BARTELLO
The devil come, and go with him.

PENURIO
The devil's come indeed, he brings your wife, Sir.

ISABELLA
We are undone, undone then.

BARTELLO
My wife with him?
Why this is a dismal day.

PENURIO
They are hard by too, Sir.

BARTELLO
I must not, dare not see her.

ISABELLA
Nor my Husband,
For twenty thousand pound.

BARTELLO
That I were a Cat now,
Or any thing could run into a Bench-hole,
Saint Anthonies Fire upon the rogue has brought her;
Where shall I be? just i'th' nick o'th' matter!
When I had her at my mercy! think for heaven sake,
My wife, all the wild furies hell has.

PENURIO
Up the Chimney.

BARTELLO
They'll smoke me out there presently.

ISABELLA
There, there, it must be there,
We are all undone else: it must be up the Chimney.

BARTELLO
Give me a Ladder.

ISABELLA
You must use your Art, Sir,
Alas, we have no Ladders.

BARTELLO
Pox o'thy Husband,
Does he never mend his house?

PENURIO
No, nor himself neither:
Up nimbly, Sir, up nimbly.

BARTELLO
Thou know'st I am fat,
Thou merciless lean rogue.

PENURIO
Will ye be kill'd?
For if he take ye—

BARTELLO
Lend me thy shoulder.

PENURIO
Soft, Sir,
You'll tread my shoulder-bones into my sides else,
Have ye fast hold o'th' barrs?

BARTELLO
A vengeance barr 'em.

ISABELLA
Patience good Captain, Patience: quickly, quickly.

BARTELLO
Do you think I am made of smoke?

PENURIO
Now he talks of smoke,
What if my Master should call for fire?

BARTELLO
Will ye Martyr me?

ISABELLA
He must needs have it.

BARTELLO
Will ye make me Bacon?

ISABELLA

We'll do the best we can, are all things ready?

PENURIO
All, all, I have 'em all.

ISABELLA
Go let 'em in then,
Not a word now on your life.

BARTELLO
I hang like a Meteor.

[Enter **LOPEZ** and **RODOPE**.

LOPEZ
You are welcome Lady.

RODOPE
You are too too courteous,
But I shall make amends, fair Isabella.

ISABELLA
Welcome my worthy friend, most kindly welcome.

RODOPE
I hear on't, and I'll fit him for his foolery.

LOPEZ
Some Sweet meats wife: some Sweet meats presently.

BARTELLO
Oh my sowre sauce.

LOPEZ
Away quick Isabella.

[Exit **ISABELLA**.

Did you hear him?

RODOPE
Yes, yes, perfectly, proceed, Sir.

LOPEZ
Speak loud enough: Dare ye at length but pity me?

RODOPE
'Faith Sir, you have us'd so many reasons to me,

And those so powerfully—

LOPEZ
Keep this kiss for me.

BARTELLO
And do I stand and hear this?

RODOPE
This for me, Sir,
This is some comfort now: Alas my Husband—
But why do I think of so poor a fellow,
So wretched, so debauch'd?

BARTELLO
That's I, I am bound to hear it.

RODOPE
I dare not lye with him, he is so rank a Whoremaster.

LOPEZ
And that's a dangerous point.

RODOPE
Upon my conscience, Sir,
He would stick a thousand base diseases on me.

BARTELLO
And now must I say nothing.

LOPEZ
I am sound Lady.

RODOPE
That's it that makes me love ye.

LOPEZ
Let's kiss again then.

RODOPE
Do, do.

BARTELLO
Do, the Devil
And the grand Pox do with ye.

LOPEZ
Do ye hear him? well—

[Enter **PENURIO** and **ISABELLA**.

Now, what's the news with you?

PENURIO
The sound of War, Sir,
Comes still along: The Duke will charge the City,
We have lost they say.

LOPEZ
What shall become of me then,
And my poor wealth?

BARTELLO
Even hang'd, I hope.

RODOPE
Remove your Jewels presently,
And what you have of wealth into the Cittadel,
There all's secure.

LOPEZ
I humbly thank ye Lady:
Penurio, get me some can climb the Chimney,
For there my Jewels are, my best, my richest,
I hid 'em, fearing such a blow.

PENURIO
Most happily:
I have two boys that use to sweep foul Chimneys,
Truly I brought 'em, Sir, to mock your worship,
For the great Fires ye keep, and the full Diet.

LOPEZ
I forgive thee knave, where are they?

PENURIO
Here Sir, here:
Monsieur Black, will your small worship mount?

[Enter two **BOYS**.

1ST BOY
Madam è be com to creep up into your Chimney, and make you

[**BOY** sings.

Cleane, as any Lady in de world: Ma litla, litla frera, and è,
Chanta, frere, chanta.

PENURIO
Come Monsieur, mountè, mountè, mount Monsieur Mustard-pot.

[**BOY** sings.

1ST BOY
Monsieur è have dis for votra barba, ple ta vou Monsieur.

PENURIO
Mountà Monsieur, mountà dere be some fine tings.

1ST BOY
Me will creep like de Ferret Monsieur.

PENURIO
Dere in the Chimney.

[The **BOY** above singing.

1ST BOY
He be de sheilde due shauson, Madam.

[**BOY** goes in behind the Arras.

PENURIO
There's a Bird's nest, I wou'd have ye climb it Monsieur,
Up my fine singing Monsieur: that's a fine Monsieur.

LOPEZ
Watch him, he do not steal.

PENURIO
I warrant ye Sir.

LOPEZ
These Boys are knavish.

BOY [Within]
Madam here be de Rat, de Rat, Madam.

PENURIO
I'll look to him tithly.

LOPEZ
Lord, what comes here,

A walking apparition?

[**BOY** sings upon **BARTELLO'S** Shoulder.

ISABELLA
Saint Christopher.

RODOPE
Mercy o' me, what is it?
How like my Husband it looks?

BARTELLO
Get ye down devil,
I'll break your neck else: was ever man thus chimnied?

LOPEZ
Go pay the boys well; see them satisfied.

PENURIO
Come Monsieur Devils, come my Black-berries
I'll butter ye o' both sides.

[**BOY** Exit [saying Adieu Madam, adieu Madam].

ISABELLA
Nay, ev'n look Sir, are you cooled now, Captain?

BARTELLO
I am cuckolled, and fool'd to boot too:
Fool'd fearfully, fool'd shamefully.

LOPEZ
You are welcome Sir,
I am glad I have any thing within these doors Sir
To make ye merry: you love my wife, I thank ye.
You have shew'd your love.

BARTELLO
Wife, am I this? this odd matter,
This monstrous thing?

RODOPE
You ought, but yet you are not:
I have been bold with you Sir, but yet not basely,
As I have faith I have not.

LOPEZ
Sir, believe it,

'Twas all meant but to make you feel your trespass;
We knew your hour, and all this fashion'd for it.

BARTELLO
Were you o'th' plot too?

ISABELLA
Yes by my troth, sweet Captain.

BARTELLO
You will forgive me wife?

RODOPE
You will deserve it?

BARTELLO
Put that to th' venture.

RODOPE
Thus am I friends again then,
And as you ne'er had gone astray, thus kiss ye.

BARTELLO
And I'll kiss you, and you too ask forgiveness,
Kiss my wife Lopez, 'tis but in jest remember;
And now all friends together to my Castle,
Where we'll all dine, and there discourse these stories,
And let him be Chimney-swept in's lust that glories.

[Exit.

SCÆNA QUARTA

Enter **SILVIO** and **BELVIDERE** severally.

SILVIO
Hail reverend Dame, heaven wait upon thy studies.

BELVIDERE
You are all well met Son: what is the Battel ended?

SILVIO
Mother, 'tis done.

BELVIDERE
How has thy honour prosper'd?

SILVIO

The Dutchess has the day, Syenna's prisoner:
Arm'd with thy powerful Art, this arm dismounted him,
Receiv'd him then on foot, and in fair valour.
Forc'd him mine own, this Jewel I took from him,
It hung upon his cask, the Victors triumph:
And to the Dutchess now a Prisoner
I have render'd him: Come off again unknown, Mother.

BELVIDERE

'Tis well done, let me see the Jewel Son;
'Tis a rich one, curious set, fit for a Princess Burgonet:
This rich Token late was sent, by the Dutchess with intent,
The Marriage next day to begin: Dost thou know what's hid within?
Wipe thine eyes, and then come near, see the beauteous Belvidere:
Now behold it.

SILVIO

Oh my Saint.

BELVIDERE

Wear it nobly, do not faint.

SILVIO

How blest am I in this rich spoil, this Picture,
For ever will I keep it here, here Mother,
For ever honor it: how oft, how chastly
Have I embrac'd the life of this, and kist it!

BELVIDERE

The day draws on that thou must home return,
And make thy answer to the Dutchess question
I know it troubles thee, for if thou fail in't.

SILVIO

Oh, I must dye.

BELVIDERE

Fear not, fear not, I'll be nigh,
Cast thy trouble on my back, Art nor cunning shall not lack,
To preserve thee, still to keep, what thy envious foemen seek;
Go boldly home, and let thy mind, no distrustful crosses find:
All shall happen for the best; souls walk through sorrows that
are blest.

SILVIO

Then I go confident.

BELVIDERE
But first my Son, a thankful service must be done,
The good old woman for her pain, when every thing stands fair again,
Must ask a poor Boon, and that granting, there's nothing to thy
journey wanting.

SILVIO
Except the trial of my soul to mischief,
And as I am a Knight, and love mine honor,
I grant it whatsoever.

BELVIDERE
Thy pure soul
Shall never sink for me, nor howl.

SILVIO
Then any thing.

BELVIDERE
When I shall ask, remember.

SILVIO
If I forget, heavens goodness forget me.

BELVIDERE
On thy journey then awhile, to the next cross way and stile,
I'll conduct thee, keep thee true, to thy Mistriss and thy vow,
And let all their envies fall, I'll be with thee, and quench all.

[Exeunt.

ACTUS QUINTUS

SCÆNA PRIMA

Enter **DUCHESS, DUKE of SYENNA**, and **LORD**.

DUKE of SYENNA
Lady, the stubborn war's more mild than you are,
That allows Ransom, and the Prisoner taken—

DUCHESS
We must not be too hasty: Remember Sir,
The wrong and violence you have offer'd us,

Burnt up our frontier Towns, made prey before ye
Both of our Beasts, and Corn; slain our dear subjects,
Open'd the fountain eyes of thousand widows,
That daily fling their curses on your fury;
What ordinary satisfaction can salve this?
What hasty thought-on Ransome give a remedy?
You must excuse us yet, we'll take more counsel:
In the mean time, not as a prisoner,
But as a noble Prince we entertain ye.

DUKE of SYENNA
I am at your mercy Lady, 'tis my fortune,
My stubborn fate; the day is yours, you have me,
The valour of one single man has cross'd me,
Crost me and all my hope; for when the Battel's
Were at the hottest game of all their furies,
And conquest ready then to crown me Victor,
One single man broke in, one sword, one vertue,
And by his great example thousands followed,
Oh how I shame to think on't, how it shakes me!
Nor could our strongest head then stop his fury,
But like a tempest 'bore the field before him,
Till he arriv'd at me, with me he buck'lled,
A while I held him play; at length his violence
Beat me from my saddle, then on foot pursu'd me,
There triumph'd once again, then took me prisoner:
When I was gone, a fear possest my people.

DUCHESS
One single arm, in a just cause, heaven prospers.
Is not this stranger Knight as yet discover'd,
That we may give his virtue a due honor?

LORD
Not yet that we hear Madam, but to that purpose,
Two daies ago we publish'd Proclamations.

[Enter **SOTO** with a Trumpet and **SILVIO**.

SOTO
Oh dainty Dutchess, here I bring that Knight
Before thy fragrant face, that warlike wight,
He that Syenna's Duke, and all his Louts
Beat (as the Proverb seemly saies) to clouts:
He that unhors'd the man o' fame to boot,
And bootless taught his Grace to walk afoot:
He that your writings (pack'd to every pillar)
Promis'd promotion to, and store of siller,

That very man I set before thy Grace,
And once again pronounce, this man it was.

DUCHESS
A pretty foolish Squire, what must the Knight be?

DUKE of SYENNA
Some Jugler or some Mad man.

SILVIO
I was not so,
When thy faint Troops in flocks I beat before me,
When, through the thickest of thy warlike horse,
I shot my self even to thy Standard Duke,
And there found thee, there singled thee, there shew'd thee
The temper of my Sword. 'Tis true, thou stoodst me,
And like a noble soldier bidst me welcome;
And this I'll say, More honor in that arme,
I found and tryed, than all thy Army carried:
What follows thy imprisonment can tell thee.

DUKE of SYENNA
His fair relation carries truth and virtue,
And by those Arms I see, (for such were his,
So old, so rusty) this may be he that forc'd me.

SILVIO
Do you know this Jewel, from your Cask I rent it,
Even as I clos'd, and forced ye from your saddle;
Do you now remember me?

DUKE of SYENNA
This is the valour
Madam, for certain he, it must be he,
That day I wore this Jewel, you remember it.

DUCHESS
Yes, very well; not long before I sent it.

DUKE of SYENNA
That day I lost this Jewel, in fight I lost it,
I felt his strokes, and felt him take it from me,
I wore it in my Cask; take it again Sir,
You won it nobly, 'tis the prize of honor.

SOTO
My Father and my self are made for ever.

DUCHESS
Kneel down brave Sir thus my Knight first I raise ye,
Gird on a Sword; next General of my Army,

[Discovers himself.

Give him a staff; last, one in Counsel near me.
Now, make us happy with your sight: how? Silvio?
Have I on thee bestow'd this love, this honor?
The Treasons thou hast wrought set off with favours?
Unarm him presently: Oh thou foul Traitor,
Traitor to me, mine honor, and my Countrey,
Thou kindler of these Wars.

SILVIO
Mistake not Madam.

DUCHESS
Away with him to prison,
See him safe kept, the Law shall shortly sirrah,
Find fitter Titles for ye, than I gave ye.

SOTO
This is the youth that kill'd me, I'll be quit with him,
What a blind rogue was I, I could never know him!
And't please your Grace, I claim the benefit
Of the Proclamation that proclaim'd him Traitor,
I brought him in.

DUCHESS
Thou shalt have thy reward for't.

SOTO
Let him he hang'd, or drown'd then.

DUCHESS
Away with him.

SILVIO
Madam, I crave your promise first; you are tyed to it,
You have past your Princely word.

DUCHESS
Prove it, and take it.

SILVIO
This is the day appointed,
Appointed by your Grace for my appearance,

To answer to the Question.

DUCHESS
I remember it.

SILVIO
I claim it then.

DUCHESS
If you perform it not,
The penalty you claim too.

SILVIO
I not repent it;
If I absolve the words?

DUCHESS
Your life is free then,
You have drawn a speedy course above my wishes,
To my revenge, be sure ye hit it right,
Or I'll be sure you shall not scape the danger.

SILVIO
My rest is up now Madam.

DUCHESS
Then play it cunningly.

SILVIO
Now, where's the Hag? where now are all her promises,
She would be with me, strengthen me, inform me?
My death will now be double death, ridiculous:
She was wont still to be near, to feel my miseries,
And with her Art, I see her no where now;
What have I undertaken? now she fails me,
No comfort now I find, how my soul staggers!
Till this hour never fear nor doubt possest me,
She cannot come, she will not come, she has fool'd me;
Sure, she is the Devil, has drawn me on to ruine,
And now to death bequeaths me in my danger.

DUKE of SYENNA
He stands distracted, and his colour changes.

DUCHESS
I have given him that will make his blood forsake him;
Shortly his life.

DUKE of SYENNA
His hands and contemplation
Have motion still, the rest is earth already.

DUCHESS
Come, will ye speak or pray? your time grows out Sir;
How every where he looks! he's at last cast.

[Enter **BELVIDERE**, and secretly gives him a paper, and Exit.

DUKE of SYENNA
His colour comes again fresh.

DUCHESS
'Tis a flash, Sir,
Before the flame burns out; can ye yet answer?

SILVIO
Yes Madam, now I can.

DUCHESS
I fear you'll fail in't.

SILVIO
And do not think my silence a presage,
Or Omen to my end, you shall not find it;
I am bred a Soldier not an Orator:
Madam, peruse this scrowl, let that speak for me,
And as you are Royal, wrong not the construction.

DUCHESS
By heaven you shall have fair play.

SILVIO
I shall look for't.

Question.
Tell me what is that only thing,
For which all women long;
Yet having what they most desire,
To have it do's them wrong.

Answer.
Tis not to be chaste, nor fair,
Such gifts malice may impair;
Richly trimm'd to walk or ride,
Or to wanton unespy'd;
To preserve an honest name,

And so to give it up to fame;
These are toys. In good or ill
They desire to have their Will;
Yet when they have it, they abuse it,
For they know not how to use it.

DUCHESS
You have answer'd right, and gain'd your life,
I give it.

SILVIO
Oh happy Hag! But my most gracious Madam,
Your promise ty'd a nobler favour to me.

DUCHESS
'Tis true, my Daughter too.

SILVIO
I hope you will keep it.

DUCHESS
'Tis not in my power now, she is long since wander'd,
Stol'n from Court, and me; and what I have not
I cannot give: no man can tell me of her,
Nor no search find her out: and if not Silvio,
Which strongly I believe—

SILVIO
Mock me not Lady,
For as I am a servant to her virtue,
Since my first hour of exile, I ne'er saw her.

LORD
That she is gone, 'tis too too true, and lamentable,
Our last hope was in you.

SILVIO
What do I hear then,
And wherefore have I life bestow'd and honor?
To what end do I walk? for men to wonder at,
And fight, and fool? pray ye take your honors from me,
(My sorrows are not fit companions for 'em)
And when ye please my life: Art thou gone Mistriss,
And wander'st heaven knows where? this vow I make thee,
That till I find thee out, and see those fair eyes;
Those eyes that shed their lights, and life into me,
Never to know a friend, to seek a kindred,
To rest where pleasure dwels, and painted glory,

But through the world; the wide world, thus to wander,
The wretched world alone, no comfort with me,
But the meer meditations of thy goodness:
Honor and greatness, thus adieu.

[Enter **BELVIDERE**.

BELVIDERE
Stay Silvio,
And Lady sit again, I come for Justice.

SILVIO
What would she now?

BELVIDERE
To claim thy promise Silvio,
The boon thou swor'st to give me.

DUKE of SYENNA
What may this be,
A Woman or a Devil?

DUCHESS
'Tis a Witch sure,
And by her means he came to untwist this Riddle.

SILVIO
That I am bound to her for my life, mine honor;
And many other thousand ways for comfort
I here confess: confess a promise too,
That what she would aske me to requite these favours,
Within the endeavour of my life to grant,
I would; and here I stand my words full master.

BELVIDERE
I wish no more: great Lady, witness with me,
The boon I crave for all my service to thee,
Is now to be thy wife, to grant me marriage.

SILVIO
How? for to marry thee? ask again woman,
Thou wilful woman, ask again.

BELVIDERE
No more Sir.

SILVIO
Ask Land, and Life.

BELVIDERE
I aske thee for a Husband.

SOTO
Marry her, and beat her into Gun-powder,
She would make rare Crackers.

SILVIO
Ask a better fortune,
Thou art too old to marry: I a Soldier,
And always married to my sword.

BELVIDERE
Thy word Fool,
Break that, and I'll break all thy fortunes yet.

DUCHESS
He shall not,
I am witness to his faith: and I'll compel it.

DUKE of SYENNA
'Tis fit ye hold your word, Sir.

SILVIO
Oh most wretched.

DUCHESS
This was a fortune now beyond my wishes,
For now my Daughter's free, if e'er I find her.

DUKE of SYENNA
But not from me.

DUCHESS
You are sharer in this happiness,
My self will wait upon this marriage,
And do the old woman all the honor possible.

DUKE of SYENNA
I'll lead the Knight, and what there wants in dalliance,
We'll take it out in drink.

SILVIO
Oh wretched Silvio.

[Exeunt.

SCÆNA SECUNDA

Enter **LOPEZ** and **ISABELLA**.

LOPEZ
Hast thou sent for him?

ISABELLA
Yes.

LOPEZ
A young man, saist thou?

ISABELLA
Yes, very young, and very amorous.

LOPEZ
And handsome?

ISABELLA
As the Town affords.

LOPEZ
And dar'st thou
Be so far good, and Mistriss of thine honor,
To slight these?

ISABELLA
For my Husband's sake to curse 'em,
And since you have made me Mistriss of my fortune,
Never to point at any joy, but Husband,
I could have cozen'd ye, but so much I love ye,
And now so much I weigh the estimation
Of an unspotted wife—

LOPEZ
I dare believe thee,
And never more shall doubt torment my spirit.

[Enter **PENURIO**.

ISABELLA
How now Penurio?

PENURIO
The thing is comming, Mistriss.

LOPEZ
I'll take my standing.

PENURIO
Do, and I'll take mine.

[Exit **LOPEZ**.

ISABELLA
Where didst thou leave him?

PENURIO
I left him in a Cellar,
Where he has paid me titely, paid me home Mistriss,
We had an hundred and fifty healths to you, sweet Mistriss,
And threescore and ten damnations to my Master;
Mistriss, shall I speak a foolish word to ye?

ISABELLA
What's that Penurio?
The fellow's drunk.

PENURIO
I would fain know your body.

ISABELLA
How's that? how's that prethee?

PENURIO
I would know it carnally,
I would conglutinate.

ISABELLA
The reason sirrah?

PENURIO
Lobster, sweet Mistriss, Lobster.

ISABELLA
Thy Master hears.

PENURIO
Lobster, sweet Master, Lobster.

ISABELLA
Thou art the most pretious rogue.

[Enter **CLAUDIO**.

PENURIO
Most pretious Lobster.

ISABELLA
Do you see who's here? go sleep ye drunken rascal.

PENURIO
Remember you refuse me arm'd in Lobster.

[Exit.

ISABELLA
Oh my lost Rugio, welcome, welcome, welcome,
A thousand welcomes here I'll seal.

CLAUDIO
Pray ye stay, Lady,
Do you love me ever at this rate? or is the fit now,
By reason of some wrong done by your Husband,
More fervent on ye?

ISABELLA
Can I chuse but love thee?
Thou art my Martyr, thou hast suffered for me,
My sweet, sweet Rugio.

CLAUDIO
Do you do this seriously?
'Tis true, I would be entertained thus.

ISABELLA
These are nothing,
No kisses, no embraces, no endearments,
To those—

CLAUDIO
Do what you will.

ISABELLA
Those that shall follow,
Those I will crown our love withal; why sigh ye?
Why look ye sad my dear one?

CLAUDIO
Nay, faith nothing,
But methinks so sweet a beauty, as yours shews to me,

And such an innocence as you may make it,
Should hold a longer Siege.

ISABELLA
Ha, you speak truth, Sir.

CLAUDIO
I would not have it so.

ISABELLA
And now methinks,
Now I consider truly what becomes me,
I have been cozen'd, fearfully abus'd,
My reason blinded.

CLAUDIO
Nay, I did but jest with ye.

ISABELLA
I'll take ye at your word, and thank ye for't Sir;
And now I see no sweetness in that person,
Nothing to stir me to abuse a Husband,
To ruine my fair fame.

CLAUDIO
Good Isabella.

ISABELLA
No handsome man, nor any thing to doat on,
No face, no tongue to catch me, poor at all points,
And I an ass.

CLAUDIO
Why do ye wrong me Lady?
If I were thus, and had no youth upon me,
My service of so mean a way to win ye,
(Which you your self are conscious must deserve ye,
If you had thrice the beauty you possess, must reach ye)
If in my tongue your fame lay wrack'd, and ruin'd
With every cup I drink: if in opinion
I were a lost, defam'd man: but this is common
Where we love most, where most we stake our fortunes,
There least and basest we are rewarded: fare ye well,
Know now I hate you too as much, contemn ye,
And weigh my credit at as high a value.

ISABELLA
May be I did but jest.

CLAUDIO
Ye are a woman,
And now I see your wants, and mine own follies,
And task my self with indiscretion,
For doating on a face so poor.

ISABELLA
Say ye so Sir,
(I must not lose my end) I did but jest with you,
Only fool'd thus to try your faith: my Rugio,
Do you think I could forget?

CLAUDIO
Nay, 'tis no matter.

ISABELLA
Is't possible I should forsake a constancy,
So strong, so good, so sweet?

CLAUDIO
A subtle woman.

ISABELLA
You shall forgive me, 'twas a trick to try ye,
And were I sure ye lov'd me—

CLAUDIO
Do you doubt now?

ISABELLA
I do not doubt, but he that would profess this,
And bear that full affection you make shew of,
Should do—

CLAUDIO
What should I do?

ISABELLA
I cannot shew ye.

CLAUDIO
I'll try thee damnedst Devil: hark ye Lady,
No man shall dare do more, no service top me,
I'll marry ye.

ISABELLA
How Sir?

CLAUDIO
Your Husband's sentenc'd,
And he shall dye.

ISABELLA
Dye?

CLAUDIO
Dye for ever to ye,
The danger is mine own.

ISABELLA
Dye did ye tell me?

CLAUDIO
He shall dye, I have cast the way.

ISABELLA
Oh foul man,
Malicious bloody man.

[Enter **LOPEZ**.

LOPEZ
When shall he dye, Sir,
By whom, and how?

CLAUDIO
Hast thou betraid me, woman?

ISABELLA
Base man, thou would'st have ruin'd me, my name too
And like a Toad, poison'd my virtuous memory:
Further than all this, dost thou see this friend here,
This only friend, shame take thy Lust and thee,
And shake thy soul, his life, the life I love thus,
My life in him, my only life thou aim'st at.

CLAUDIO
Am I catcht thus?

LOPEZ
The Law shall catch ye better.

ISABELLA
You make a trade of betraying Womens honors,
And think it noble in ye to be lustful,

Report of me hereafter—

CLAUDIO
Fool'd thus finely?

LOPEZ
I must intreat ye walk, Sir, to the Justice,
Where if he'll bid ye kill me—

CLAUDIO
Pray stay awhile, Sir,
I must use a Players shift, do you know me now Lady?

LOPEZ
Your brother Claudio sure.

ISABELLA
Oh me, 'tis he Sir,
Oh my best brother.

CLAUDIO
My best sister now too,
I have tryed ye, found ye so, and now I love ye,
Love ye so truly nobly.

LOPEZ
Sir, I thank ye,
You have made me a most happy man.

CLAUDIO
Thank her Sir,
And from this hour preserve that happiness,
Be no more fool'd with jealousie.

LOPEZ
I have lost it,
And take me now new born again, new natur'd.

ISABELLA
I do, and to that promise tye this faith,
Never to have a false thought tempt my virtue.

LOPEZ
Enough, enough, I must desire your presence,
My Cosin Rodope has sent in all haste for us,
I am sure you will be welcome.

CLAUDIO

I'll wait on ye.

LOPEZ
What the Project is—

ISABELLA
We shall know when we are there, Sir.

[Exeunt.

Enter **DUCHESS, DUKE of SYENNA, LORDS, SILVIO**.

DUCHESS
Joy to you Silvio, and your young fair Bride,
You have stolen a day upon us; you cannot wooe, Sir.

SILVIO
The joyes of Hell hang over me, oh mischief,
To what a fortune has the Devil driven me!
Am I reserv'd for this?

DUKE of SYENNA
Beshrew me, Sir,
But you have gotten you a right fair bedfellow,
Let you alone to chuse.

SILVIO
I beseech your Grace,
'Tis misery enough to have met the Devil,
Not mens reproaches too.

DUKE of SYENNA
How old is she?

DUCHESS
A very Girl, her eye delivers it.

DUKE of SYENNA
Her teeth are scarce come yet.

LORD
What goodly children
Will they two have now! she is rarely made to breed on,
What a sweet timber'd body!

DUCHESS
Knotty i' th' back,
But will hold out the stronger; What a nose!

DUKE of SYENNA
I marry, such a nose, so rarely mounted,
Upon my conscience, 'twas the part he doted on.

DUCHESS
And that fine little eye to it, like an Elephant's.

LORD
Yes, if her feet were round, and her ears sachels.

DUKE of SYENNA
For any thing we know.

SILVIO
Have ye no mercy?
No pity in your bloods to use a wretch thus?
You Princes in whose hearts the best compassions,
Nearest to those in Heaven, should find fit places,
Why do you mock at misery? fling scorns and baseness
Upon his broken back, that sinks with sorrows?
Heaven may reward you too, and an hour come,
When all your great designes shall shew ridiculous,
And your hearts pinch'd like mine.

[Musick in divers places.

DUCHESS
Fie Sir, so angry
Upon your wedding day? go smug your self,
The Maid will come anon: what Musick's this?

DUKE of SYENNA
I warrant you some noble preparation.

DUCHESS
Let's take our places then.

SILVIO
More of these Devils dumps?
Must I be ever haunted with these witchcrafts?

[Enter a Masquerado of several shapes, and Dances, after which, enter **BELVIDERE** and disperses them; before the **MASKERS** enter two **PRESENTERS**, among which are **BARTELLO, LOPEZ, CLAUDIO, ISABELLA, RODOPE, SOTO, PENURIO, JAQUENET.**

1ST PRESENTER
Room, room for merry spirits, room,
Hither on command we come,
From the good old Beldam sent,
Cares and sorrows to prevent.

2ND PRESENTER
Look up Silvio, smile, and sing,
After winter comes a Spring.

1ST PRESENTER
Fear not faint fool what may follow,
Eyes that now are sunk and hollow,
By her Art may quick return
To their flames again, and burn.

2ND PRESENTER
Art commands all youth, and blood,
Strength and beauty it makes good.

1ST PRESENTER
Fear not then, despair not, sing
Round about as we do spring:
Cares and sorrows cast away,
This is the old wives Holy-day.

[Dance here, then enter **BELVIDERE.**

DUCHESS
Who is this?

DUKE of SYENNA
The shape of Belvidere.

BELVIDERE
Now Silvio,
How dost thou like me now?

SILVIO
Thus I kneel to thee.

BELVIDERE
Stand up, and come no nearer, mark me well too,
For if thou troublest me, I vanish instantly:

Now chuse wisely, or chuse never,
One thou must enjoy for ever.
Dost thou love me thus?

SILVIO
Most dearly.

BELVIDERE
Take heed fool, it concerns thee nearly.
If thou wilt have me young and bright,
Pleasing to thine eye and sight,
Courtly, and admir'd of all,
Take heed lest thy fame do fall,
I shall then be full of scorn,
Wanton, proud, beware the horn,
Hating what I lov'd before,
Flattery apt to fall before,
All consuming, nothing getting,
Thus thy fair name comes to setting.
But if old, and free from these
Thou shalt chuse me, I shall please:
I shall then maintain thee still,
With my virtue and my skill
Still increase and build thy name,
Chuse now Silvio here I am.

SILVIO
I know not what to say, which way to turn me,
Into thy Soveraign will I put my answer.

BELVIDERE
I thank ye Sir, and my Will thus rewards ye,
Take your old Love, your best, your dearest Silvio:
No more Spells now, nor further shapes to alter me,
I am thy Belvidere indeed. Dear Mother,
There is no altering this; heavens hand is with it:
And now you ought to give me, he has fairly won me.

SILVIO
But why that Hag?

BELVIDERE
In that shape most secure still,
I followed all your fortunes, serv'd, and counsell'd ye,
I met ye at the Farmers first, a Countrey wench,
Where fearing to be known, I took that habit,
And to make ye laughing sport at this mad marriage,
By secret aid of my friend Rodope

We got this Maske.

SILVIO
And I am sure I have ye.

BELVIDERE
For ever now, for ever.

DUCHESS
You see it must be,
The wheel of destiny hath turn'd it round so.

DUKE of SYENNA
It must, it is, and curs'd be he that breaks it.

DUCHESS
I'll put a choice to you, Sir: ye are my prisoner.

DUKE of SYENNA
I am so, and I must be so, till it please you—

DUCHESS
Chuse one of these, either to pay a Ransom,
At what rate I shall set it, which shall be high enough,
And so return a Free-man, and a Batchelor,
Or give me leave to give you a fit wife,
In honor every way your Graces equal,
And so your Ransom's paid.

DUKE of SYENNA
You say most nobly,
Silvio's example's mine, pray chuse you for me.

DUCHESS
I thank ye Sir, I have got the mastry too,
And here I give your Grace a Husbands freedom:
Give me your hand, my Husband.

DUKE of SYENNA
You much honor me,
And I shall ever serve ye for this favour.

BARTELLO
Come Lopez, let us give our wives the breeches too,
For they will have 'em.

LOPEZ
Whilst they rule with virtue

I'll give 'em, skin and all.

ISABELLA
We'll scratch it off else.

SILVIO
I am glad ye live, more glad ye live to honor,
And from this hour a stronger love dwell with us;
Pray you take your man again.

CLAUDIO
He knows my house, Sir.

DUCHESS
'Tis sin to keep you longer from your loves,
We'll lead the way; and you young men that know not
How to preserve a wife, and keep her fair,
Give 'em their soveraign Wills, and pleas'd they are.

John Fletcher – A Short Biography

John Fletcher was born in December, 1579 in Rye, Sussex. He was baptised on December 20th.

As can be imagined details of much of his life and career have not survived and, accordingly, only a very brief indication of his life and works can be given.

His father, Richard Fletcher, was a successful and rather ambitious cleric. From being the Dean of Peterborough he moved on to become the Bishop of Bristol, Bishop of Worcester and finally, shortly before his death, the Bishop of London. He was also the chaplain to Queen Elizabeth.

When he was Dean of Peterborough, Richard Fletcher, witnessed the execution of Mary, Queen of Scots. It was said he "knelt down on the scaffold steps and started to pray out loud and at length, in a prolonged and rhetorical style, as though determined to force his way into the pages of history". He cried out at her death, "So perish all the Queen's enemies!" All very dramatic but the family did have strong links to the Arts.

Young Fletcher appears at the very young age of eleven to have entered Corpus Christi College at Cambridge University in 1591. There are no records that he ever took a degree but there is some small evidence that he was being prepared for a career in the church.

However what is clear is that this was soon abandoned as he joined the stream of people who would leave University and decamp to the more bohemian life of commercial theatre in London.

Unfortunately his father fell out with Queen Elizabeth but appears to have been on his way to rehabilitation before his death in 1596. At his death he was, however, mired in debt.

The upbringing of the now teenage Fletcher and his seven siblings now passed to his paternal uncle, the poet and minor official Giles Fletcher. Giles, who had the patronage of the Earl of Essex may have been a liability rather than an advantage to the young Fletcher. With Essex involved in the failed rebellion against Elizabeth Giles was also tainted by association.

By 1606 John Fletcher appears to have equipped himself with the talents to become a playwright. Initially this appears to have been for the Children of the Queen's Revels, then performing at the Blackfriars Theatre.

Commendatory verses by Richard Brome in the Beaumont and Fletcher 1647 folio place Fletcher in the company of Ben Jonson, although it is not known when this friendship began. Jonson, of course, was a leviathan of English Literature, so admired that many of his literary friends and colleagues were simply known as 'Sons of Ben'. Fletcher's frequent early collaborator, Francis Beaumont, was also a friend of Jonson's.

Fletcher's early career was marked by one significant failure; The Faithful Shepherdess, his adaptation of Giovanni Battista Guarini's Il Pastor Fido, which was performed by the Blackfriars Children in 1608. In the preface to the printed edition of his play, Fletcher explained the failure as due to his audience's faulty expectations. They expected a pastoral tragicomedy to feature dances, comedy, and murder, with the shepherds presented in conventional stereotypes – as Fletcher put it, wearing "gray cloaks, with curtailed dogs in strings." Fletcher's preface is however best known for its pithy definition of tragicomedy: "A tragicomedy is not so called in respect of mirth and killing, but in respect it wants [i.e., lacks] deaths, which is enough to make it no tragedy; yet brings some near it, which is enough to make it no comedy." A comedy, he went on to say, must be "a representation of familiar people." His preface is critical of drama that features characters whose action violates nature.

In that case, Fletcher appears to have been developing a new style faster than audiences could comprehend. By 1609, however, he had found his stride. With Beaumont, he wrote Philaster, which became a hit for the King's Men and began a profitable association between Fletcher and that company. Philaster appears also to have begun a trend for tragicomedy. Fletcher's influence has also been said to have inspired some features of Shakespeare's late romances, and certainly his influence on the tragicomic work of other playwrights is even more marked.

By the middle of the 1610s, Fletcher's plays had achieved a popularity that rivalled Shakespeare's and cemented the pre-eminence of the King's Men in Jacobean London. After Beaumont's retirement, necessitated by ill-health, and then his early death in 1616, Fletcher continued working, both singly and in collaboration, until his death in 1625. By that time, he had produced, or had been credited with, close to fifty plays. This body of work remained a major part of the King's Men's repertory until the closing of the theatres in 1642 due to the Civil War.

At the beginning of his career Fletcher's most important collaborator was Francis Beaumont. The two wrote together for close to a decade, first for the Children of the Queen's Revels, and then for the King's Men. According to an anecdote transmitted or invented by John Aubrey, they also lived together in Bankside, sharing clothes and having "one wench in the house between them." This domestic arrangement, if it existed, was ended by Beaumont's marriage in 1613, and their dramatic partnership ended after Beaumont fell ill, probably of a stroke, that same year.

At this point Fletcher had written many plays with Beaumont and several others on his own. He seems to have been regarded as quite a talent although it should be remembered that playwrights were required to be prolific, to easily work with other collaborators and to produce work of quality and commercial appeal very quickly.

The King's Men, run by Philip Henslowe, was the most prestigious of the theatre companies and Fletcher now had an increasingly close association with it.

Fletcher collaborated with Shakespeare on Henry VIII, The Two Noble Kinsmen, and the now lost Cardenio, which some scholars say was the basis for Lewis Theobald's play Double Falsehood. (Theobald is regarded as one of the best Shakespearean editors. Whether his play is based on Cardenio or on some other is not absolutely known although Theobald certainly promoted it as his revision of the lost Shakespeare/Fletcher play.)

A play that Fletcher also wrote by himself at this time, The Woman's Prize or the Tamer Tamed, is also regarded as a sequel to The Taming of the Shrew.

In 1616, with the death of Shakespeare, Fletcher now appears to have entered into an enhanced arrangement with the King's Men on very similar terms to Shakespeare's. Fletcher would now write exclusively for the King's Men until his own death almost a decade later.

As well as continuing his solo productions Fletcher was still collaborating with other playwrights, mainly Philip Massinger, who, in turn, would succeed him as the in-house playwright for the King's Men.

Fletcher's popularity continued throughout his life; indeed during the winter of 1621, he had three of his plays performed at court. His mastery is most notable in two dramatic types; tragicomedy and the comedy of manners.

John Fletcher died in 1625, it is thought of bubonic plague which, at the time, was undergoing further outbreaks.

He seems to have been buried in what is now Southwark Cathedral, although a precise location is not known. There is much made of an anecdote that Fletcher and Massinger (who died in 1640) share the same grave but it is more likely that both are buried within a few yards of each other and that the stone markers in the floor have confused the issue. One is marked 'Edmond Shakespeare 1607' and the other 'John Fletcher 1625' refers to Shakespeare's younger brother and the playwright. The churchyards were, more often than not, completely over-crowded and breeding grounds for disease. Precise record keeping was not a practiced skill.

During the later Commonwealth, many of the playwright's best-known scenes were kept alive as drolls. These were brief performances, usually condensed into one or two scenes and with the addition of music or song to satisfy the taste for plays while the theatres were closed under the Puritans. At the re-opening of the theatres in 1660, the plays in the Fletcher canon, in original form or revised, were by far the most common productions on the English stage. The most frequently revived plays suggest the developing taste for comedies of manners. Among the tragedies, The Maid's Tragedy and, especially, Rollo Duke of Normandy held the stage. Four tragicomedies (A King and No King, The Humorous Lieutenant, Philaster, and The Island Princess) were popular, perhaps in part for their similarity to and foreshadowing of heroic drama. Four comedies (Rule a Wife And Have a Wife, The Chances, Beggars' Bush, and especially The Scornful Lady) were also stage mainstays.

Despite his popularity, and it appears he was held in higher regard than Shakespeare at this time, his works steadily lost ground to those of Shakespeare and to new productions from other playwrights.

Since then Fletcher has increasingly become a subject only for occasional revivals and for specialists. Fletcher and his collaborators have been the subject of important bibliographic and critical studies, but the plays have been revived only infrequently.

Due to the frequent collaborations between all manner of playwrights, and the revisions carried out in later years, having a settled list of authorship to any given set of plays can be problematic. The works of Fletcher and others of this period most definitely fall into this category. It is as well to take into account that during this period theatres were quite often closed either due to outbreaks of the plague or to the prevailing political and moral climate. Printers, anxious to provide materials that would sell, were not above changing a name or two to enhance sales.

Although Fletcher collaborated most often with Beaumont and Massinger, it is believed that Massinger revised many of the plays some time after their original production. Other collaborators including Nathan Field, William Shakespeare, William Rowley and others also can be seen distinctly in Fletchers' works. Many modern scholars point out that Fletcher had many particular mannerisms but other playwrights would also duplicate these at times so allocating exact contributions of anyone to a play is somewhat of a detective case in many instances. However from the original folio printings or licensing via the Master of the Revels (the statutory licensing authority to approve and censor plays as well a hand in publication and printing of theatrical materials) as well as contemporary notes a fairly precise bibliography of the works can be given with only a few plays lacking substantial authority and provenance.

John Fletcher – A Concise Bibliography

This bibliography gives the most likely date of writing together with when published, revised or licensed by the Master or the Revels (This position within the royal household was originally for royal festivities, ie revels, and later to oversee stage censorship, until this function was transferred to the Lord Chamberlain in 1624).

Solo Plays
The Faithful Shepherdess, pastoral (written 1608–9; printed 1609)
The Tragedy of Valentinian, tragedy (1610–14; 1647)
Monsieur Thomas, comedy (c. 1610–16; 1639)
The Woman's Prize, or The Tamer Tamed, comedy (c. 1611; 1647)
Bonduca, tragedy (1611–14; 1647)
The Chances, comedy (c. 1613–25; 1647)
Wit Without Money, comedy (c. 1614; 1639)
The Mad Lover, tragicomedy (acted 5 January 1617; 1647)
The Loyal Subject, tragicomedy (licensed 16 November 1618; revised 1633; 1647)
The Humorous Lieutenant, tragicomedy (c. 1619; 1647)

Women Pleased, tragicomedy (c. 1619–23; 1647)
The Island Princess, tragicomedy (c. 1620; 1647)
The Wild Goose Chase, comedy (c. 1621; 1652)
The Pilgrim, comedy (c. 1621; 1647)
A Wife for a Month, tragicomedy (licensed 27 May 1624; 1647)
Rule a Wife and Have a Wife, comedy (licensed 19 October 1624; 1640)

Collaborations

With Francis Beaumont
The Woman Hater, comedy (1606; 1607)
Cupid's Revenge, tragedy (c. 1607–12; 1615)
Philaster, or Love Lies a-Bleeding, tragicomedy (c. 1609; 1620)
The Maid's Tragedy, Tragedy (c. 1609; 1619)
A King and No King, tragicomedy (1611; 1619)
The Captain, comedy (c. 1609–12; 1647)
The Scornful Lady, comedy (c. 1613; 1616)
Love's Pilgrimage, tragicomedy (c. 1615–16; 1647)
The Noble Gentleman, comedy (c. 1613; licensed 3 February 1626; 1647)

With Francis Beaumont & Philip Massinger
Thierry & Theodoret, tragedy (c. 1607; 1621)
The Coxcomb, comedy (c. 1608–10; 1647)
Beggars' Bush, comedy (c. 1612–13; revised 1622; 1647)
Love's Cure, comedy (c. 1612–13; revised 1625; 1647)

With Philip Massinger
Sir John van Olden Barnavelt, tragedy (August 1619; MS)
The Little French Lawyer, comedy (c. 1619–23; 1647)
A Very Woman, tragicomedy (c. 1619–22; licensed 6 June 1634; 1655)
The Custom of the Country, comedy (c. 1619–23; 1647)
The Double Marriage, tragedy (c. 1619–23; 1647)
The False One, history (c. 1619–23; 1647)
The Prophetess, tragicomedy (licensed 14 May 1622; 1647)
The Sea Voyage, comedy (licensed 22 June 1622; 1647)
The Spanish Curate, comedy (licensed 24 October 1622; 1647)
The Lovers' Progress or The Wandering Lovers, tragicomedy (licensed 6 December 1623; rev 1634; 1647)
The Elder Brother, comedy (c. 1625; 1637)

With Philip Massinger & Nathan Field
The Honest Man's Fortune, tragicomedy (1613; 1647)
The Queen of Corinth, tragicomedy (c. 1616–18; 1647)
The Knight of Malta, tragicomedy (c. 1619; 1647)

With William Shakespeare
Henry VIII, history (c. 1613; 1623)
The Two Noble Kinsmen, tragicomedy (c. 1613; 1634)

Cardenio, tragicomedy (c. 1613)

With Thomas Middleton & William Rowley
Wit at Several Weapons, comedy (c. 1610–20; 1647)

With William Rowley
The Maid in the Mill (licensed 29 August 1623; 1647).

With Nathan Field
Four Plays, or Moral Representations, in One, morality (c. 1608–13; 1647)

With Philip Massinger, Ben Jonson and George Chapman
Rollo Duke of Normandy, or The Bloody Brother, tragedy (c. 1617; revised 1627–30; 1639)

With James Shirley
The Night Walker, or The Little Thief, comedy (c. 1611; 1640)
The Coronation c. 1635

Uncertain
The Nice Valour, or The Passionate Madman, comedy (c. 1615–25; 1647)
The Laws of Candy, tragicomedy (c. 1619–23; 1647)
The Fair Maid of the Inn, comedy (licensed 22 January 1626; 1647)
The Faithful Friends, tragicomedy (registered 29 June 1660; MS.)

The Nice Valour is possibly by Fletcher revised by Thomas Middleton;

The Fair Maid of the Inn is perhaps a play by Massinger, John Ford, and John Webster, either with or without Fletcher's involvement.

The Laws of Candy has been variously attributed to Fletcher and to John Ford.

The Night-Walker was a Fletcher original, with additions by Shirley for a 1639 production.

Even now there is not absolute certainty on several of the plays. The first Beaumont & Fletcher folio of 1647 contained 35 plays and the second folio of 1679 added a further 18. In total 53 plays.

The first folio included The Masque of the Inner Temple and Gray's Inn (1613), and the second The Knight of the Burning Pestle (1607), widely considered Beaumont's solo works, although the latter was in early editions attributed to both writers. Fletcher himself said that Beaumont was attributed so-authorship of many works that belonged solely to Fletcher or to other collaborators.

One play in the canon, Sir John Van Olden Barnavelt, existed in manuscript and was not published till 1883.

www.ingramcontent.com/pod-product-compliance
Lightning Source LLC
Chambersburg PA
CBHW060118050426
42448CB00010B/1930